The Jerry Rescue

CRITICAL HISTORICAL ENCOUNTERS

Series Editors
James Kirby Martin
David M. Oshinsky
Randy W. Roberts

The Jerry Rescue

The Fugitive Slave Law, Northern Rights, and the American Sectional Crisis

ANGELA F. MURPHY

Texas State University

New York   Oxford

OXFORD UNIVERSITY PRESS

Oxford University Press is a department of the University of Oxford.
It furthers the University's objective of excellence in research, scholarship,
and education by publishing worldwide.

Oxford   New York
Auckland   Cape Town   Dar es Salaam   Hong Kong   Karachi
Kuala Lumpur   Madrid   Melbourne   Mexico City   Nairobi
New Delhi   Shanghai   Taipei   Toronto

With offices in
Argentina   Austria   Brazil   Chile   Czech Republic   France   Greece
Guatemala   Hungary   Italy   Japan Poland   Portugal   Singapore
South Korea   Switzerland   Thailand   Turkey   Ukraine   Vietnam

Copyright © 2016 by Oxford University Press

Published by Oxford University Press
198 Madison Avenue, New York, New York 10016
http://www.oup.com

Oxford is a registered trademark of Oxford University Press

Library of Congress Cataloging-in-Publication Data
Murphy, Angela F., 1967-
    The Jerry rescue : the Fugitive Slave Law, Northern rights, and the American sectional
crisis / Angela F. Murphy.
        pages cm. -- (Critical historical encounters)
    Includes bibliographical references and index.
    ISBN 978-0-19-991360-2 (paperback : alkaline paper) 1. Fugitive slaves--New York
(State)--Syracuse--History--19th century. 2. United States. Fugitive slave law (1850)
3. Rescues--New York (State)--Syracuse--History--19th century. 4. Loguen, Jermain
Wesley. 5. May, Samuel J. (Samuel Joseph), 1797-1871. 6. Underground Railroad--
New York (State)--Syracuse. 7. Antislavery movements--Northeastern States--
History--19th century. 8. Slavery--Political aspects--United States--History--19th century.
9. Sectionalism--United States--History--19th century. 10. United States--Politics and
government--1845-1861. I. Title.
    E450.M87 2016
    326'.80974766--dc23

                                                                                    2014029428

Printing number: 9 8 7 6 5 4 3 2 1

Printed in the United States of America
on acid-free paper

For Richard Blackett

CONTENTS

························

EDITOR'S FOREWORD

The volumes in this Oxford University Press book series focus on major critical encounters in the American experience. The word *critical* refers to formative, vital, transforming events and actions that have had a major impact in shaping the ever-changing contours of life in the United States. *Encounter* indicates a confrontation or clash, often but not always contentious in character, but always full of profound historical meaning and consequence.

In this framework, the United States, it can be said, has evolved on contested ground. Conflict and debate, the clash of peoples and ideas, have marked and shaped American history. The first Europeans transported with them cultural assumptions that collided with Native American values and ideas. Africans forced into bondage and carried to America added another set of cultural beliefs that often were at odds with those of Native Americans and Europeans. Over the centuries America's diverse peoples have differed on many issues, often resulting in formative conflict that in turn has given form and meaning to the American experience.

The Critical Historical Encounters series emphasizes formative episodes in America's contested history. Each volume contains two fundamental ingredients: a carefully written narrative of the encounter, and the consequences, both immediate and long-term, of that moment of conflict in America's contested history.

One of the most divisive problems in the history of the United States was the sectional dispute over the continued existence of chattel slavery within the nation after American independence. From the nation's founding through the Civil War, the gradual eradication of slavery in the Northern states coincided with its expansion in the South, contributing to a sectional divide that invaded American politics—a divide that eventually led to the fracturing of the American nation. Sectional politics in the United States became especially contentious following a war with Mexico that in 1848 added a vast amount of new territory to the nation. The opening of this territory raised the question of the expansion of slavery into these new lands and forced Americans into debates about the future of that institution in the American republic. American politicians attempted to find a compromise that would satisfy both Northern and Southern interests in the Compromise of 1850, which addressed, among other matters, Northern concerns about the expansion of slavery into the West as well as Southern demands for a tougher Fugitive Slave Law. Instead of quelling sectional tensions, the Compromise of 1850 helped to set in motion a series of events that sharpened the divide between the North and South. The rescue of a fugitive slave named Jerry from federal custody in Syracuse, New York, on October 1, 1850, was one of these events.

Among the most provocative features of the compromise that followed the U.S.–Mexican War was the Fugitive Slave Law of 1850, which made the federal government responsible for the return of fugitive slaves who had escaped from the South and required Northern citizens to lend aid in this process when called to do so. Northern black and white abolitionists agitated against the law and seized upon Northern resentments of this expansion of federal power in order to encourage the growth of antislavery sentiment throughout the Northern states. Some Northern citizens were converted and joined the abolition movement. Others remained unconcerned about slavery as a Southern institution but became anxious about the way that slaveholder demands had precipitated an infringement upon their own rights. A third group encouraged obedience to the law for the sake of the American Union.

The story of Jerry's rescue illustrates the various positions that Northerners held concerning the Fugitive Slave Law and shows the way in which the controversial nature of that law played a strong role in the growth of sectional tensions throughout the 1850s. The following narrative is the first book-length treatment of this episode of resistance to the Fugitive Slave Law. Utilizing the voices of those who were involved in the events, historian Angela F. Murphy's *The Jerry Rescue: The Fugitive Slave Law, Northern Rights, and the American Sectional Crisis* investigates the controversial policies that sparked resistance to the law. In addition, this study provides an engaging description of the rescue itself and examines the ways in which abolitionists used the event to further their antislavery agenda in upstate New York and elsewhere. In sum, this captivating volume illuminates the centrality of the fugitive slave issue in energizing Northern debates about the place of slavery in the nation as those differences contributed to the sectional divide over slavery that would eventually culminate in civil war.

James Kirby Martin
David M. Oshinsky
Randy W. Roberts

On Clinton Square in downtown Syracuse stands a monument to the Jerry Rescue. Erected in 1990, it memorializes an episode in which a group of people in the town proudly resisted the execution of a federal law. With claims about individual liberty, Northern states' rights, and the need to privilege God's laws over those of human beings, they effectively nullified the Fugitive Slave Law of 1850 within Syracuse borders.

A bronze statue set in the monument celebrates the forcible liberation of Jerry, a fugitive from slavery who was arrested by federal officials on October 1, 1851, and who, under the terms of the new law, was likely to be re-enslaved. In the center of the statue stands Jerry, bare-chested and shackled, running away from his captors. Flanked on either side of him are two of Syracuse's most prominent abolitionists: Samuel J. May, a white Unitarian minister who was affiliated with the American Anti-Slavery Society, and Jermain Wesley Loguen, a black fugitive from slavery who led the effort to aid other runaway slaves who came through town. As they pause by the monument, Syracuse residents can proudly reflect on their town's antislavery past and upon its connection to the Northern network to aid fugitive slaves known as the Underground Railroad.

The Jerry Rescue is an important piece of Syracuse history, but it also has national significance. The story of the rescue, and the related events that preceded and followed it, illuminate the way that the

The Jerry Rescue Monument on Clinton Square in Syracuse. Jerry is in in the middle, with Samuel J. May behind him on the left and Jermain Loguen behind him on the right.
Angela F. Murphy

institution of slavery inserted itself into the sectional politics of the young American republic and into the lives of American residents. It reveals much about the Northern movement to end slavery and the choices that both antislavery activists and ordinary citizens made in the face of what many considered to be an immoral American law. It highlights the cooperation of black and white residents who worked together in defiance of the law, but often in widely different ways and for widely different reasons. Finally, it shows how disagreements over policies concerning fugitive slaves contributed to the sectional divide between the slave and the free states that eventually led to disunion and the Civil War.

My aim in this book is to connect this bit of Syracuse history to the larger historical narrative of the American sectional crisis of the 1850s. The story in the following pages therefore ranges from the halls of Congress to the antislavery meeting houses of upstate New York to the streets of Syracuse. It includes in its cast of characters those relegated to the lowest positions in American society alongside middle-class reformers and the most powerful American politicians.

Bringing all of these elements of the story together not only highlights the way in which an important local event relates to the national narrative; it also shows how American laws can profoundly affect the lives of individuals and how individual actions can affect American political conversations. American lawmakers and party leaders of the nineteenth century debated the issue of slavery in political and ideological terms, and in our historical examinations of those debates the human dimension of political decision-making often is lost. The story of the Jerry Rescue, however, emphasizes the personal stakes involved in the politics of slavery. It demonstrates how slave law affected Americans of all stripes: black and white, Northern and Southern, rich and poor, male and female, powerful and powerless. And it shows how the decisions made by individuals affected the course of history.

This book thus can be seen as not only a microhistory that connects a specific event to the larger historical narrative but also as a collective biography of sorts. Although the Jerry Rescue Monument depicts three of the central actors in the story of the Syracuse resistance to the Fugitive Slave Law, there are many others who have important roles in the Jerry Rescue story: supporters of the antislavery Liberty Party who were meeting in Syracuse on the day of Jerry's arrest; diverse members of the Syracuse black community who banded together in self-protection; women who opposed slavery but who also worried about the fate of family members who took risks in order to resist American slave law; Syracuse residents who were not previously affiliated with the antislavery movement but were angry over the law's intrusion into their lives; local federal officials who had to deal with the conflict surrounding Jerry's arrest; and national politicians whose legislation affected these individuals. All of their stories are here.

Because my work highlights the experiences of individuals involved in the events surrounding the rescue, I have relied heavily on the voices of these historical participants to tell its story. First person accounts in letters, diaries, and memoirs shape the narrative. In addition to these personal accounts, information from contemporary newspapers—which include editorials, correspondence and reports of various meetings and trials—were invaluable in shedding light on the reactions to the Fugitive Slave Law and the Jerry Rescue in both Syracuse and other parts of the nation. Finally, Congressional and judicial records reveal the national debates on slavery and the Fugitive Slave Law that frame the story of the rescue. Of course secondary works produced by other scholars also have informed this narrative. In addition to sources mentioned in the endnotes, readers will find a list of works that were especially influential in my understanding of this book's major issues in the section entitled "For Further Reading." I am indebted to all of the scholars who produced these works.

I also am indebted to the local historians of the Onondaga Historical Association who over the years have collected and organized a vast amount of material on the Jerry Rescue and made it available in their research center in downtown Syracuse. Among other items, they have preserved newspaper clippings, legal documents, and photos. The OHA houses valuable resources that provide not only information on the Jerry Rescue and the antislavery activities of the city but also on conservative groups in the city who opposed what they saw as attacks on American institutions that endangered the social order. In addition, its holdings contain material that highlight the experiences of both ordinary and extraordinary white and black Syracusans. I owe a special thanks to Sarah Kozma, the center's research specialist, who helped me locate materials and who made copies of documents so that I could maximize my time in Syracuse. Thanks go out, as well, to Texas State University's Research Enhancement Program, which provided a grant that funded travel and research expenses for the project.

I also want to thank friends who encouraged and provided feedback on the project. Texas State colleagues Ana Romo and Paul Hart were part of a writing group that helped me to gather momentum in the early stages of my research and writing. Ana was also helpful later in the writing process, reading through a draft of the manuscript and talking through ways to effectively revise the work. Head of the history department, Mary Brennan, ensured that I had research release time to work on the book. Other friends who provided encouragement and advice include Theresa Jach, Marjorie Brown, Leigh Fought, Douglas Egerton, and A. J. Aiserithe. Beverly Tomek, who read through a late draft of the work, was especially helpful. My husband Ned Murphy also read through multiple iterations of the work and cheered me along as I wrote.

I am grateful to James Martin and to Brian Wheel who have allowed this study to stand alongside works of other distinguished writers who have contributed to the Critical Historical Encounters Series at Oxford University Press. Thanks go out as well to those who reviewed the work for the press and provided feedback, including Ana Lucia Araujo, Amy S. Greenberg, James L. Huston, Anne E. Marshall, and Thomas Summerhill.

Because this is a book meant to be used in the classroom, it is appropriate that my most enthusiastic expressions of gratitude are offered to an influential teacher and to my own students. First I must thank Richard Blackett for inspiring my interest in the Jerry Rescue. Richard—who later became my dissertation adviser, mentor, and friend—taught the first research seminar that I took as a doctoral student at the University of Houston in the fall of 2000. The semester assignment: to write a research paper on reactions to the Fugitive Slave Law of 1850 in a Northern town of our choosing. I chose Syracuse. That very first paper I wrote at the University of Houston turned, with encouragement from Richard, into my first article publication. It also sparked my interest in the antislavery movement, which is now the emphasis of my own scholarship.

I went on to write about other topics, but the project from this research seminar stayed with me. It not only encouraged my interest in the antislavery movement, but it opened my eyes to how important the Northern resistance to the Fugitive Slave Law was in the dynamics of the American sectional crisis. I found myself referring to the story I uncovered in Syracuse in the courses that I taught on antebellum America and on the Civil War at Texas State University. Each time I recounted the story, I found new ways in which it spoke to the larger issues that drove mid-nineteenth-century American history, and indeed, to many issues that still concern us today. Ten years after writing that first graduate paper, I finished my first book, and it was easy to settle on my next project: a history of the Jerry Rescue and its aftermath. It would be a microhistory that could shed light on the larger issues involved in the coming of the Civil War. It would be written with my students in mind.

It is my hope, however, that this work resonates with scholars as well as with students and lay readers. Although the following account is written primarily for a general audience and traces themes that are familiar to historians of the sectional crisis, I believe that my study of the issues and events surrounding the Jerry Rescue also makes a contribution to the historical scholarship of that crisis. It highlights the way that reactions to the Fugitive Slave Law became intertwined with the concern over the expansion of slavery in the West and shows the complicated dynamics of the fracturing of the Union. It reveals the role that abolitionists played in encouraging resistance to American slave law, and it adds nuance to our understanding of abolitionist debates about violent resistance, the constitutionality of slavery, and the dynamics of race. Its focus on upstate New York brings much-needed attention to the role of the Liberty Party within the abolitionist movement and highlights just how organized and how "above ground" the operations of the Underground Railroad were in that region. Finally, this first book-length treatment of the Jerry Rescue brings the Syracuse rescue story alongside other more well-known episodes of resistance to the Fugitive Slave Law, giving the event its due as a critical historical encounter in the American narrative. It deserves such notice, for it was the first successful biracial rescue that gained national attention after the passage of the Fugitive Slave Law of 1850, and the issues associated with the event set the stage for later debates over the Fugitive Slave Law, slavery, and sectional politics that took place in the years before the Civil War.

INTRODUCTION

....

I t happened on October 1, 1851.

Jerry was making barrels at Morell's Cooperage when his world changed. The rest of Syracuse was crowded and preoccupied that Wednesday morning, but it was just a normal work day for the middle-aged, black employee of Frederic Morell. As he bent his head, incongruously covered with a shock of red hair, over his workbench, an air of excitement hung over the central New York town. Syracuse was packed with thousands of visitors. Some were there to attend the Onondaga County Agricultural Fair near Hanover Square. Others were attending the Liberty Party Convention that was meeting at the town's First Congregational Church. Syracuse was bustling, but it was quiet at the cooperage, and Jerry's plan was to go about his usual routine. The other workmen had left the shop to go to lunch, so Jerry had the place to himself.

His solitude, however, was soon interrupted. Around noon, a group of federal marshals, led by Henry W. Allen and aided by local police officers, entered the shop. Jerry was at his workbench with his back to the door, and the lawmen came up behind him, threw him to the floor, and placed him in handcuffs. Once they had him secured, Allen informed Jerry that he was under arrest. Jerry had committed no crime, but he had already had his share of trouble with the law, and he knew the drill by now. He had been arrested several times over the previous two years—once for theft and three other times for assault and battery, a result of his heated relationship with Sarah Colwell.[1] Based on his past experiences, Jerry knew that it was best to cooperate and clear the matter up rather than try to resist.

Jerry surely would have been less compliant, however, had he known the real reason he was detained.[2] The officers were not arresting him for theft or assault. They had seized Jerry under the terms of the new Fugitive Slave Law of 1850, which required the federal government to help return those who had fled from Southern slavery to those who claimed the fugitives as property. Jerry, who had seized his freedom and undergone great hardship to maintain his liberty, was to be re-enslaved.[3]

Jerry's arrest sparked a reaction in Syracuse that would for a time bring the city front and center into the American republic's heated debates on how slavery, which prospered in the Southern states but had gradually come to an end in the states of the North, affected the American Union. Members of Congress had passed the Fugitive Slave Law of 1850 as part of a compromise on slavery that was meant to keep the divided republic whole. A particularly intense debate had taken place in the Senate over the details of this compromise, with men like John Calhoun and Jefferson Davis representing Southern interests and men like William Seward asserting Northern unwillingness to comply with Southern demands that the institution of slavery must be protected everywhere in the nation. Into the sectional breach stepped Henry Clay and Daniel Webster, who insisted that a compromise regarding slavery must be made between the free North and the slave South for the sake of the Union. The resulting legislation, the Compromise of 1850, would affect all Americans. On October 1, 1851, it would especially affect the town of Syracuse.

Charles Wheaton, owner of a nearby hardware store, was passing by Morell's Cooperage when he saw the officers leading Jerry out onto the street in chains. Wheaton was an antislavery man and a member of the town's biracial Vigilance Committee—a body formed in order to protect fugitives from slavery who had settled in Syracuse. Wheaton sprung to duty when he saw that Jerry was in trouble. He rushed to the Congregational Church where he informed delegates of the Liberty Party that federal officers had arrested Jerry. The Liberty Party was organized around antislavery principles, and Wheaton was himself a member of it. In the crowd gathered at the church he knew he would find men sympathetic to Jerry's fate.

Gerrit Smith, who presided over the convention, immediately adjourned the proceedings when Wheaton arrived with his news. Smith would be a powerful ally for Jerry. The wealthy philanthropist was one of the leading lights of the antislavery movement in the state of New York. His home in nearby Peterboro was a refuge for many who had escaped slavery, and he was one of the loudest critics of the Fugitive Slave Law. After the convention's adjournment, Smith and the other delegates rushed to the office of federal commissioner Joseph F. Sabine, where the marshals had taken Jerry to hear his fate. According to the reminiscences of Liberty Party member Jermain Loguen, "Their procession was a signal of alarm to the throng which they passed—stopping only as they met a friend to explain themselves, and plant a kindred feeling." He described the scene: "The young and active led the way—the strong and middle aged followed with elevated brow and firm tread—age-stiffened limbs brought up the rear—and the faces of all, relieved of every shadow that would obscure the brilliancy of their indignation, were attracted to the chained slave in the commissioner's office."[4]

From this moment on, Gerrit Smith and other members of the Liberty Party would take a special interest in Jerry's case. Among those who were most active was John Thomas, who edited an antislavery

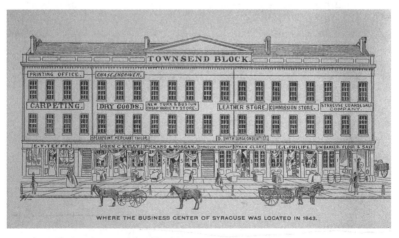

Woodcut of the Townsend Block Building, where Federal Commissioner Joseph Sabine held an office in 1851.
From the Collection of the Onondaga Historical Association, 321 Montgomery Street, Syracuse, NY 13202

newspaper with Rochester abolitionist and famed fugitive slave Frederick Douglass. Thomas would document the story of Jerry's arrest for *Frederick Douglass' Paper*. Jermain Loguen was also active on Jerry's behalf. Loguen, like Jerry, had escaped from Southern slavery and taken up residence in Syracuse. And like Frederick Douglass, Loguen was an outspoken abolitionist and advocate for Northern black men and women. He was also the town's foremost agent of the Underground Railroad. Joining Loguen in his protest of Jerry's arrest was fellow black Liberty Party member Samuel Ringgold Ward, a Syracuse resident who had spent recent months traveling through the Northern states, giving speeches against the Fugitive Slave Law of 1850.

The news of Jerry's arrest spread through the city, and soon church bells were ringing out, a signal prearranged by the Vigilance Committee to let Syracuse residents know that a fugitive had been arrested. Samuel J. May, the minister of the town's Unitarian Church and an active member of the American Antislavery Society, heard the signal, and he also rushed to take a place by Jerry's side. He was happy to see other members of the Syracuse community heading in the same direction. "The nearer I got to the place," May recalled in his memoirs, "the more persons I met, all excited, many of them infuriated by the thought that a man among us was to be carried away into slavery."[5] As the bells pealed, a great crowd assembled in front of the Townsend Block Building at the corner of Water and Clinton Street, where Commissioner Sabine kept his second floor office.

John Thomas described the scene he found as he arrived at Sabine's office in his report for *Frederick Douglass' Paper*. It was "the most revolting and cruel sight I ever beheld," he began. He described Jerry, the "poor colored man," as a "strong, bony, muscular fellow" who was clad only in a check shirt and trousers and sitting in chains in the back of the room. James Lear, a "brawny Kidnapper from Missouri," was present and "armed to the teeth." Lear served as the agent of Jerry's alleged owner, John McReynolds. McReynolds had sent Lear to secure Jerry's return to slavery. Also present were District Attorney James R. Lawrence, who aided Lear in presenting his claim; Commissioner Sabine, who was to conduct a hearing to consider Jerry's status; and Leonard Gibbs, an attorney from Washington County who was in town for the Liberty Party meeting. Gibbs had volunteered to serve as Jerry's counsel. A "bevy of constables" and federal marshals were also present as were many onlookers, black and white, who had pressed into the room to view the proceedings. The office, Thomas said, was "wedged full with human bodies."[6]

When they arrived at Sabine's office, Gerrit Smith and Samuel J. May both took a place by Jerry's side in order to provide him with guidance and moral support. Jermain Loguen also pushed into the room in order to protest Jerry's arrest—a bold move since the man was a fugitive from slavery himself. Samuel Ringgold Ward was just arriving in town from a lecture tour as the excitement took place, and he would join up with his colleagues later in the day.

All of these men, along with many other men and women present in the town of Syracuse on that autumn afternoon, would soon take part in an episode that would have repercussions not only for Jerry, but also for the town and, indeed, the nation as a whole. After Jerry's arrest, many in Syracuse challenged the validity of the Fugitive Slave Law of 1850 and attempted to prevent its enforcement. Others insisted that the law of the land must be obeyed and that the Compromise of 1850 must be preserved for the sake of the nation. The debates in Syracuse over Jerry's arrest in 1851 were thus connected to the larger debates about the nature of the American Union and the compromise legislation enacted by Congress in its name the previous year. As residents of Syracuse and its environs considered their obligations within a republic that protected slavery, a nation riven by sectional discord watched the drama in the town play out.

Life for Jerry changed when he was arrested, but it also changed for Jerry's advocates. And this transformation was part of a larger national story of upheaval set during the 1850s—a decade during which a series of events provoked the destruction of an old order that recognized the legitimacy of slavery in the United States and a decade that would end in civil war. The events set in motion by Jerry's arrest on October 1, 1851—and the stories of those who participated in them—are part of the chronicle of that upheaval.

CHAPTER 1

....

Sectionalism and Slavery

On the day of his arrest, Jerry had resided in Syracuse for almost two years. There he had joined a black community of around 350 people—a small proportion in a town that numbered around 22,000.[1] Members of this community had varied backgrounds. Some of the older men and women had been slaves before New York lawmakers made slavery illegal in the state in 1827. Others were the descendants of those who had been enslaved before emancipation. A smaller group consisted of fugitives like Jerry who had fled from bondage in the South where slavery remained entrenched.

Jerry had been lucky. Most of America's three million Southern slaves had no hope of escape from an institution that robbed them of control over their own fates. As the Northern states had gradually emancipated their slaves following the American Revolution, the system of slavery had expanded in the South and slave owners maintained a tight grip on their captive laborers. The best hope for those born into Southern slavery in the early nineteenth century was an escape to free territory, a feat very few were able to pull off.[2]

Over time, however, there were hints that things could change. During the first half of the nineteenth century, more Americans in free states began to question how slavery fit into the American nation. Black Americans, of course, had always been the most vocal critics of slavery. As time progressed, they were joined by white abolitionists who questioned the morality of the institution. These abolitionists always remained a small minority in the North, but by the middle of the 1850s they were joined by other white Americans who believed that the expansion of slavery within the borders of the United States impinged upon white rights and inhibited white upward mobility by circumscribing opportunities for free laborers.

The existence of slavery in the South and its absence in the North thus provoked sectional tension during the years of the early republic as political and economic leaders became increasingly divided concerning the future of the American nation. Would it be a republic that allowed slavery, or would a dedication to free labor characterize its development? Would there be a permanent sectional divide between slavery and freedom in the United States, or would the nation be able to unite—becoming either wholly free or wholly supportive of slavery?

While American leaders debated these questions, the nation remained divided, with millions enslaved. During this time, fugitives like Jerry increasingly sought refuge in the Northern states, hoping to lead independent lives and control their own destinies. Those in Syracuse were especially hopeful, for they were just about as far from the boundary between slavery and freedom that one could get and still remain within the nation.

Jerry himself was hopeful. After he arrived in Syracuse in the winter of 1849/1850, he decided to remain in the city. He was able to find work there and establish some personal connections. He had reasonable hope for upward mobility in Syracuse, but this does not mean that life was easy. Although slavery no longer existed in the Northern town, and although many residents had begun to adopt antislavery views, racial prejudice was rampant there, as it was in all the Northern states.

Jerry's initial experiences in Syracuse illustrate the divided nature of the town and indeed of the free states of the North. His first place of employment in Syracuse was with a cabinet maker named Charles F. Williston. Williston, who would later in the decade serve as the city's mayor, was a liberal Democrat who opposed the expansion of slavery in the nation. He was a member of Samuel J. May's Unitarian church—a church that promoted antislavery principles—and he participated actively in antislavery organizations. When Jerry arrived in Syracuse, Williston hired him to work the lathe in his shop, where he employed around forty-five other workers. At the end of Jerry's first week, however, members of the cabinet shop's workmen's committee visited Williston and told him that "the nigger must quit," or his other workers would walk out. Williston held firm. He told the committee that the workers were free to leave. It was his shop; he had hired Jerry, and Jerry would stay. Jerry remained at the cabinet shop for over a year, and, according to Williston, eventually became a "favorite." Jerry kept abreast of the politics of the nation, including slave policy, and Williston had newspapers delivered to the shop just for his reading. When Jerry left Williston's shop to work at Morrell's cooperage in 1851, it was his own decision. He left in order to make better wages.[3] Thus, despite real difficulties, Jerry had found some measure of control over his destiny in Syracuse.

Jerry's initial troubles with Williston's employees, however, illustrate the racial prejudice that African Americans faced even in the free North. Although the state of New York had ended slavery by the time that Jerry arrived in Syracuse, most people in the region still considered black people inferior to whites. Evidence of this sentiment abounded in the town. For example, after the construction of a concert hall in Syracuse in the early 1850s, minstrel shows became a popular pastime for many city residents. These shows, in which white men painted their faces black and depicted stereotypical versions of African Americans, were advertised even in newspapers like the *Syracuse Standard* that promoted antislavery principles. The *Standard* announced in its pages shows with "counterfit niggers" and "distinguished 'culled pussons.'" The blackface performers "are considerable more nigger than the darkey himself," one advertisement bragged as it enticed readers to "go and see the fun and hear the music."[4] Another way in which racism was evident in the town was through its police activity. Jerry's own trouble with the law after he arrived in Syracuse was not unusual for members of the town's free black community. Black men were especially likely to be arrested for various minor infractions, and the newspapers of the era contain numerous announcements of their arrests for offenses like drunkenness, petty theft, assault, fighting, and cheating at cards.[5]

Despite his past legal troubles and the existence of racial prejudice within the community, Jerry had hoped to make a home in Syracuse. Following his arrest by the federal marshals, however, it became clear to Jerry that even in the state of New York, he was not free from the grasp of slavery. After he was seized as a fugitive slave, he had little chance of maintaining his freedom in Syracuse. The only way for Jerry to ensure his liberty was to escape to the safety of British Canada, where he would be beyond the legal reach of the Missouri man who claimed him as his slave. After he was seized by the federal marshals, Jerry begged those around him for their help in making an escape. He loudly proclaimed that he would do anything to avoid being returned to Missouri and re-enslaved.[6]

Sparking even greater anxiety was the possibility of being sold down the Mississippi River to the nightmare of plantation slavery in the Lower South. Runaway slaves who were brought back to their owners in Missouri often met such a fate. Deemed too troublesome to keep, owners sold them to plantations in states like Louisiana and Mississippi where the cotton economy was expanding and there was a huge demand for slave labor. Although slavery in Missouri was a harsh institution, most of the slaves brought there did not work in the labor gangs on the plantations that are so often associated with antebellum slavery. They usually worked as hands on smaller farms, as Jerry himself had, or as domestic slaves. The specter of sale "down the river," where work was dangerous and depleting and where a slave would be forever separated from friends and family was, however, often threatened by white Missourians in order to encourage slave obedience.[7] The hardships associated with plantation slavery thus cast a shadow that constantly hung over all slaves, including Jerry.

• • •

The expansion of the cotton economy and the parallel expansion of plantation slavery in the Lower South were part of larger changes that had taken place in the United States in the decades after the War of 1812—a war that had helped to encourage national growth in both the geographical and economic realms. Jerry, who was born into slavery in North Carolina in 1811, came of age as American society underwent seismic shifts. After the War of 1812, a "transportation revolution" occurred as Americans constructed new roads, canals, and, eventually, railroads that linked the various regions of the nation together. These changes helped to lead to the development of a more expansive market economy that allowed Americans to do business with those who lived far away. They also encouraged Americans to push further west into new territories, spurring the nation's continental growth.

The new interconnectedness and expansiveness led to paradoxical developments in the United States. They fostered a sense of nationalism among Americans, but they also led to conflict between the Northern and Southern states. Even as the Northern and Southern economies became more interdependent during this period, they became ever more distinct. While the Northern economy modernized and industrialized, many Southerners focused on expanding cotton cultivation, which supplied the raw material for the Northern and European textile mills that were central to industrialization.

Although Southerners chose to concentrate on agriculture rather than industry, the expansion of cotton was itself a response to the massive changes of the early nineteenth century. The growth of the market economy, along with technological innovations like the cotton gin, had made the agricultural pursuits of Southerners enormously profitable. During the first decades of the nineteenth century the desire to cultivate more cotton led to a massive push westward through the Lower South: first through Alabama, then Mississippi, and then into Louisiana and finally the eastern part of Texas. With the expansion of cotton came the expansion of slavery, and a vigorous internal slave trade developed as slaves were transported from regions less dependent on plantation agriculture to the newly settled areas. The development of this trade significantly worsened an already harsh institution, as slaves were constantly under the threat of being sold away from friends and family to fuel the demand for field labor in the Lower South.[8]

Jerry thus grew up during a time that held the promise of greater autonomy and upward mobility for many white Americans but denied that promise to most of the nation's black residents. As many American citizens looked toward a bright future, Southern slaves had no reason to feel such optimism. The engines of prosperity that created such possibilities in the nation had simultaneously strengthened the iron hand of slavery in the Southern states. If those like Jerry who were born into the institution of slavery wanted the freedom to improve their own condition—to have their own taste of the American Dream—they had to seize it themselves. And even after they did so, they could have the fruits of all of their efforts snatched from them by slave-catching officials operating with the sanction of the federal government.

• • •

Large scale western migration was not just limited to those wishing to establish cotton plantations in the Lower South in the early nineteenth century. Waves of migrants from the North and the Upper South also moved west during these years, hoping to better their circumstances by establishing farms in a region where land was more fertile and abundantly available than in their homes to the east. Migrants from the Northern states hoped that the new lands to the west would provide them with a chance to achieve economic independence through their own labor and that of hired help. Free labor was key to their vision. Many of those who were from slave-owning states, however, brought their slaves with them to supplement their efforts. Jerry's owner, William Henry, was one such migrant.

Jerry, with his red hair and light skin tone, was most likely the son of William Henry. While he was known as "Jerry" to his personal acquaintances, he is referred to as "William Henry" in official records.[9] Jerry's mother was a slave woman named Ciel, whom Henry had acquired when he married a widow from a neighboring family named McReynolds in North Carolina. Eventually both the Henry family and members of the McReynolds family would move west to Missouri.

Jerry was just a boy of around the age of seven when Henry packed up his household and left Buncombe County, North Carolina, in 1818. The Henry family settled in Marion County, Missouri, with the hope that farming the rich soil along the Mississippi River would lead to prosperity. Jerry, and the labor he would provide, was part of William Henry's plan for success. As he grew older Jerry proved to be a great asset to Henry. He became a highly skilled carpenter and cooper, and he was especially well known for crafting chairs. Jerry also was well-read and often assisted Henry in business matters. After Jerry's escape, when asked how the fugitive had been treated in the Henry household, Henry's son-in-law Joshua Gentry replied that he was treated as most Southern slaves are treated: "We direct them to go and to come; give them clothes; treat . . . them in all respects [as] subservient to the will and wishes of their masters."[10]

When William Henry brought Jerry to Missouri, slavery was already established there. Their arrival, however, coincided with a controversy over the institution's future in the region. When Missouri applied for statehood in 1819, most Missouri residents assumed that their new state would enter the union with the slave system intact, but Missouri's application led some in free states to fear that the expansion of slavery into new regions would limit the ability of white men and women to compete with slaveholding landowners. These tensions led to a political firestorm surrounding Missouri's acceptance into the Union. Young Jerry didn't know it, but the debate over Missouri statehood in 1819 and 1820 would be of great importance to his own fate. During those years, his future status as a slave or as a free man rested in the hands of politicians in Washington, DC.[11]

The crisis surrounding Missouri's bid to enter the Union was part of a conflict that had been brewing since the republic was formed. When the Founding Fathers produced the American Constitution, the Northern states were beginning the process of gradually ending

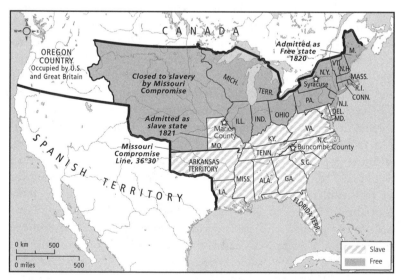

Map showing the terms of the Missouri Compromise. Marked are Jerry's birthplace in North Carolina, the location where he was enslaved in Missouri, and Syracuse, New York, where he resided in October 1851.
Map by Alliance USA

slavery. Southern leaders, however were unwilling to bring an end to a labor system that was so central to their economic prosperity. The continuation of slavery in the United States therefore was sanctioned in the Constitution, and there was a general acceptance of the idea that policies concerning slavery should be decided by state law and not by the federal government. Slavery was to be considered a "local institution." As Northern states made slavery illegal, Southern states passed laws that strengthened the slave system.

Up until Missouri's application for statehood, new states had been admitted into the United States in such a way that a sectional balance of representatives from the North and from the South had been maintained in the American Senate. The entry of Missouri would upset this balance in favor of the South, and many citizens of Northern states were concerned about an increase in Southern political power. In their eyes, the South already held disproportionate power in the federal government due to the inflation of Southern representatives in the House of Representatives and the Electoral College. Because a portion of a state's representation was based on the nonvoting slave population, the political influence of white Southerners indeed far exceeded their numbers. Now, just as Northern population growth was allowing Northerners to gain more influence in the House of Representatives, the addition of a new slave state would give Southerners control over the Senate. Furthermore, Missouri would be the first state besides Louisiana itself, which had been admitted as a slave state in 1812, to be created out of the Louisiana Purchase territory. Northerners thus feared that Missouri would set a precedent for the rest of the unorganized federal territories, over which there was no provision concerning slavery. A congressman from New York, James Tallmadge, caused a stir when he responded to these Northern concerns and attached an amendment to the Missouri statehood bill. His amendment would provide for a ban on the introduction of any new slaves in Missouri and require the gradual emancipation of slaves that already resided there. Had the Tallmadge Amendment passed, it would have set young Jerry on the course to freedom.

The amended bill, however, had little chance of success. It passed the House of Representatives, where the growing population of the Northern states gave the free states more representatives and a political advantage; but in the Senate, it was repeatedly struck down. This was possible because the South held an equal number of seats as the North and could usually rely on a few Northern senators who represented constituencies with economic ties to the South to back their interests. Thus a political standoff over the issue of Missouri statehood took place, and for the next year the nation debated what to do about the stalemate. Many Americans from free states argued that Congress was within its rights to demand that slavery be abolished as part of the terms of statehood. Southerners disagreed. They argued that such an attempt on the part of Congress would attack the property rights of slaveholders and would contradict the agreement that slavery was a state and not a federal issue. Furthermore, they asserted that the South would be politically marginalized if slavery were banned from new states entering the Union.

In 1820, politicians found a compromise that would ease the crisis. The population of Maine, an area that had been part of Massachusetts up to this point, had submitted its own petition for statehood. If Congress admitted Maine as a free state, Missouri could be admitted with slavery, and the sectional balance in the Senate would be preserved. In February 1820, the Senate passed the Missouri Compromise, which provided for the admission of both of these states to the Union—Maine without slavery and Missouri with it. In addition, an amendment was added to this compromise that prohibited slavery in the rest of the Louisiana Purchase territory north of Missouri's southern border, along the 36°30' line of latitude. While slavery was banned in the territories above that line, it would be allowed below it. At first the House of Representatives rejected this plan, but Speaker of the House Henry Clay was able to push through the major provisions of the compromise by breaking them down into three separate bills. The Missouri Compromise was thus completed, and Missouri became a "peninsula of slavery in free territory."[12] Under its terms, Jerry had no hope of freedom as long as he remained in Missouri.

• • •

The Missouri Compromise eased sectional tensions for a time, but they would not disappear. The Missouri Crisis, Thomas Jefferson said, was a "fire bell in the night"—a warning that the issue of slavery was a dangerously divisive one for the American nation.[13] Jefferson was right. The crisis was indeed a warning, for as Americans added new territories to the Union in later years, sectional antagonisms concerning slavery and political representation would resurface, forcing Americans to search for new compromises regarding the place of slavery in the nation.

While white Americans debated how slavery affected the political stability and the ideological purity of the United States, black Americans, who were locked out of this debate, would be the ones most profoundly affected by its results. Jerry himself is an example of this. Condemned to a lifetime of slavery by the Missouri Compromise, he would have to flee from the state in order to gain his freedom.

CHAPTER 2

Fugitive Slave Law

In 1843 Jerry ran. After making his way north across the Missouri state line, he moved from town to town, always fearful that his whereabouts might be discovered. Jerry's initial path to freedom was most likely along the Mississippi River through Quincy, Illinois, which was only twelve miles north of Hannibal, the largest town in Marion County. This small distance was the difference between slavery and freedom for Jerry, for Illinois was carved out of the old Northwest Territory, which had excluded slavery in 1787. It had entered the American union as a free state, and there enslaving a fellow human being was illegal.

Once Jerry crossed into free territory, however, he did not stop running. There was still the danger that he would be located and returned to slavery. Although the Missouri Compromise had set up a geographical boundary for slavery, American law concerning fugitive slaves made that boundary permeable. A slave owner could cross into free territory at any time and re-enslave fugitives who had seized their liberty. Indeed, after Jerry had escaped from Missouri, William Henry tried to find his former slave for several years, dispatching his son-in-law, Joshua Gentry, to bring Jerry home each time there was a rumor of his whereabouts. Gentry failed to capture him twice, once in Chicago and another time in Milwaukee.[1] Constitutionally, slave owners had a right to reclaim their human property from free territory within the United States, but there was little official support given to them in the execution of the slave catching process before 1850. Thus, retrieving Jerry had proved to be a difficult proposition.

Image of a male adult slave escaping by river.
Photographs and Prints Division, Shomburg Center for Research in Black Culture, The New York Public Library, Astor, Lenox and Tilden Foundations

After several disappointments, Henry gave up the search, and in July 1845 he sold Jerry *in absentia* to a man named Thomas S. Miller for $400. Soon after the sale, Henry died.[2] Several years later, Henry's step-son John McReynolds, who owned a farm just outside Hannibal, purchased Miller's claim to Jerry for the same price. The transaction took place on July 18, 1851, after the U.S. Congress passed the Fugitive Slave Law of 1850—an act that would remove many of the obstacles Southerners faced in their efforts to hunt down and bring back fugitive slaves.[3]

The specifics of Jerry's journey North and his evasions of capture before the federal marshals caught up to him in Syracuse are lost to history. Indeed, although Jerry's name is an important one in the story of how the Fugitive Slave Law of 1850 affected Americans, much of what we know about him concerns the actions that others took on his behalf in Syracuse. It is important to remember, however, that Northern activity on behalf of the fugitive slave emerged in response to actions taken by the fugitives themselves. Flight was not

just a personal act, taken at great risk, but also a political one that
defied oppressive laws concerning slavery and, increasingly, forced
Northern Americans to reconsider the idea that its citizens were dis-
connected from the institution of slavery.[4] In order to understand the
political stakes of slave escape, it is important to understand the legislation that fugitive slaves, and their supporters, defied.

• • •

The right of slaveholders to retrieve their slaves from neighboring
states was codified in Article IV, Section 2 of the United States
Constitution. This provision was not that controversial at the Constitutional Convention of 1787, for delegates had already implicitly recognized the right to human property in other parts of the document.
They had agreed upon the Three-Fifths Compromise, which allowed
that fraction of the slave population to be counted to determine a
state's population and its apportionment of representatives; and they
had agreed to Southern demands for a provision that delayed any
talk of suspending the international slave trade until 1808. The
Fugitive Slave Clause was added with little debate and was passed
unanimously.[5]

Although the Northern states were moving in the direction of
emancipation in 1787, the fact that the institution of slavery would
provoke such controversy between the Northern and Southern states
within just a few decades was not yet evident. Nearly all the states of
the proposed Union still had some individuals who were legally enslaved. In the state of New York, where Jerry would eventually take
refuge, slavery was still legal when the Constitutional Convention
met. Within the borders of New York and New Jersey, around
30,000 people labored under slavery in 1787, and one year after the
Constitutional Convention, New York would enact a new slave code
that *strengthened* the bonds of slavery there.[6] In sum, the idea of a free
North and a slave South had not yet taken shape in 1787. With slavery
still in existence on Northern soil, the right of slave owners to retrieve
their human property across state lines was not yet contested.

Even so, Southern delegates who represented slaveholder interests at the Constitutional Convention insisted that the right of
rendition—the right to demand that fugitives be handed over to a

claimant—be explicitly addressed in the Constitution. They recognized that the natural rights rhetoric of the American Revolution was eroding support for slavery in those areas of the republic that were less dependent on slave labor, and they sought to bolster the slaveholder's rights. Southerners had recently lost much of their valuable slave property during the American Revolution, as slaves ran to British lines in return for their freedom, and so the risk and cost of slave flight was very much on their minds.

In addition, a British court case that had taken place in 1772 had alerted American slave owners to the tenuous nature of their hold over their slave property. In the case of *Somerset v. Stewart*, the British High Court had upheld a claim to freedom by James Somerset, a slave who had been taken to the British Isles by his Virginia owner, Charles Stewart. Although Stewart's claim on Somerset's service was well-documented and sanctioned by Virginia law, Somerset's status on the free soil of Great Britain was in doubt. The decision of the court was that slavery could only exist by "positive law" and that accordingly Somerset had acquired his freedom once he arrived in Great Britain. Under British law, then, a slave became free once he set foot on free soil.[7] Southerners looked at the process of emancipation taking place throughout the North, and they wanted to insure that no such interpretation of slave law would flourish in the United States.

With the addition of the Fugitive Slave Clause, the Constitution made it clear that slavery would not only be tolerated in states that recognized the institution but that even in states that made slavery illegal, the slaveholder's right to human property must be accepted. Thus, although slavery was considered a state matter in both the North and the South, the Constitution clearly circumscribed free states from completely rejecting the institution, even as the Northern emancipations were carried out. The slaveholder's right to property trumped any notion that African Americans in free states had achieved permanent liberty due to state laws prohibiting slavery.

After the Constitutional Convention, the North and the South moved even further apart. Between 1787 and 1804, more Northern states embraced emancipation, and as slavery waned throughout the North the new free states became a refuge for fugitive slaves from the South. Although Southern slave owners constitutionally had the right to retrieve runaway slaves from free states, Northerners increasingly were disinclined to cooperate with rendition efforts. By the turn of the century, a humanitarian network emerged in order to protect runaway slaves from slave catchers and to help them start new, free lives. In the late eighteenth century, this network was made up primarily of members of the free black community and some anti-slavery Quakers, but it would expand over time as more slaves made their way North, more Northern white citizens adopted antislavery attitudes, and the threat of slave catchers became more prominent. By the mid-nineteenth century a name had been given to this network—the "Underground Railroad."

Many of the fugitive slaves who made use of this network were destined for Canada, where British law declared them free. Over time, however, as more Northerners became committed to ensuring their safety, more fugitives elected to make their homes in the free states, strengthening the free black communities that had taken shape there following the Northern emancipations. Jerry was one such individual.

As the Northern network to aid fugitives emerged at the end of the eighteenth century, Southerners became incensed at the failure of the Northern population to do what they argued was their constitutional duty—to surrender up fugitives to those who claimed their service. Although the Constitution was clear on the right of owners to retrieve slaves, it did not provide any sort of guidelines for how that right was to be enforced. This ambiguity would set the stage for interstate conflict as more citizens in the Northern states rejected the institution of slavery and grew less cooperative with slave owners seeking the return of fugitives.

American lawmakers became convinced that a more explicit policy needed to be codified into law in order to clarify the constitutional obligations regarding the rendition of fugitives. Congress thus passed the Fugitive Slave Act of 1793, which set up a process for the retrieval of fugitive slaves. According to the law, a claimant could go before any local, state or federal magistrate and obtain a certificate of removal that would allow him to return the fugitive to slavery. The law also made it an offense to obstruct attempts at rendition or to hide fugitives.[8]

As historian Don E. Fehrenbacher has pointed out, the Fugitive Slave Law of 1793 was an exercise in centralized power that transformed the right of recaption from a private endeavor to one that had to be facilitated by government officials. The rendition of fugitives became "a matter of federal relationship, with the national government becoming in the end virtually an agent of the slave-holding interest within free state jurisdictions."[9]

Rather than putting an end to the interstate controversies over fugitive slaves, the Fugitive Slave Law of 1793 opened the door to a new level of conflict that centered on the federal government's complicity in slavery and on whether states could be forced to participate in the perpetuation of what many increasingly considered an immoral and oppressive labor system and many more considered to be a prop that allowed a Southern oligarchy to flourish. Northern state governments sought ways to shield themselves from such participation, and they responded with state legislation to protect free black residents within their borders.

"Personal liberty laws" emerged, providing accused fugitives with the right of *habeas corpus* and trial by jury and, in some cases, instituting penalties for the unlawful imprisonment of free blacks. The passage of these laws was consistent with the generally accepted idea that slavery was a state, not a national, question; but instead of using this argument to protect the institution within the borders of slave states, as was done throughout the South, Northern leaders emphasized their states' rights to reject the claims of slaveholders in the face of a hated federal law that catered to slaveholder interests.

In addition to asserting state power over fugitive policies, the personal liberty laws were also meant to protect the black inhabitants of the free states. The Fugitive Slave Law had made them all vulnerable to kidnappers and slave catchers who sought to transport them to the South for profit, and state legislatures promoted the new laws as essential measures for the protection of their liberty. New York was the first state to pass a law specific to this issue. In 1808 it passed "An Act to Prevent the Kidnapping of Free People of Color," which instituted severe penalties, including up to fourteen years in jail, for kidnapping a free black person or removing an accused fugitive without due process.[10] Personal liberty laws made it more difficult for slave owners to retrieve fugitives, and they also made slave catchers and kidnappers vulnerable to harsh legal penalties for violating state laws.

As antislavery sentiment grew, and as resentment of Southern slaveholder dominance of federal policy concerning slavery increased in the aftermath of the Missouri Crisis, Northern states became more determined to enforce their personal liberty laws. During the 1830s, there emerged what Steven Lubet has called an "ideological antislavery bar" in the North, made up of lawyers who used the court system to interfere with slaveholder claims. They sought to use the law to slowly wear away at the power of slaveholders and to assert the rights of Northern citizens to declare that their states were not complicit in the institution of slavery.[11] In short, they wanted to make it clear that slavery was a Southern and not a national institution.

The Northern personal liberty laws rendered efforts to enforce the Fugitive Slave Law of 1793 ineffective, and so they fed into the sectional conflict over slavery. Northern states claimed that their laws trumped the provisions of the federal Fugitive Slave Law, and Southerners complained that the Northern states were ignoring federal law. Southern slaveholders worried incessantly about a broader Northern attack on slavery, and they became more vocal in their defense of the institution. That the personal liberty laws were emerging at the same time that the Missouri Crisis led to sectional controversy over the extension of slavery exacerbated Southern fears. Thus, as Northern states passed their personal liberty laws, there were loud complaints from the South that they were unconstitutional.

In 1842 these arguments made their way to the Supreme Court in the case of *Prigg v. Pennsylvania*, which addressed the constitutionality of both the Fugitive Slave Law of 1793 and the Northern personal liberty laws. In this case, Southern interests argued explicitly for the supremacy of federal over state law, while a Northern state asserted its state's right to institute protections for its black residents.

Judge Joseph Story wrote the Supreme Court's opinion on the case. In it, he upheld the constitutionality of the Fugitive Slave Law, arguing that the fugitive clause of the Constitution was a "fundamental article, without the adoption of which the Union could never have been formed." This argument was an articulation of the "historical necessity doctrine" that had emerged in American legal theory in the early nineteenth century. Essentially the argument was that the Union would not have been possible without constitutional compromises on slavery, and therefore those accommodations must be upheld.

In addition, Story asserted that slaves were defined as property. It was thus a violation of constitutional property rights for states to enact any policy that "interrupts, limits, delays or postpones the right of the owner to the immediate possession of the slave."[12] The court's ruling allowed Southern states to impose their own laws on slavery on the citizens of a Northern state. Unless a black detainee could prove he was free, Northerners had to accept the idea that he was legally a slave.

The Supreme Court's decision also, however, gave Northerners a weapon they could wield against Southern interests. Story explicitly stated that it was not constitutionally in the state's jurisdiction to return fugitive slaves but was instead under the purview of the federal government. Thus, the ruling in favor of federal over state power actually worked to the benefit of Northern states wishing to divorce themselves from the business of returning fugitives. The states did not have to participate in the process. Northern legislatures exploited this distinction, passing a new wave of personal liberty laws that forbade state officials from aiding in the rendition of slaves and that barred the use of state prisons and buildings for the imprisonment of fugitives. These new personal liberty laws made it difficult for Southerners to successfully retrieve fugitive slaves because there were few federal officials in place in the North and no federal jails. Without state facilities and aid, Southerners were left virtually on their own.

The New York state government was among the most defiant in the aftermath of the *Prigg* ruling. Governor William Seward responded to the decision with a speech to the state legislature. In it, he asserted his continued belief in the state's privilege to uphold its residents' rights to a fair trial. New York's original personal liberty laws remained on the books, despite Story's opinion.[13]

Although many hoped that the Supreme Court's decision would quell the sectional turmoil over fugitive slaves, the decision of the court actually contributed to more tension between Northerners and Southerners. Without state aid, slave owners had no significant public resources to call upon in their efforts to retrieve runaway slaves. Thus, although fugitives like Jerry were technically vulnerable to re-enslavement under the Fugitive Slave Law of 1793, Northern state laws forbidding the use of local resources to aid in the capture of fugitives and protecting the rights of accused fugitives allowed them some measure of confidence that they would remain at liberty.

Southerners were frustrated by the new personal liberty laws that sprung up in the aftermath of the *Prigg* decision. Many Northerners were also unhappy, for they resented Story's interpretation of law. Although they were able to enact new personal liberty laws under the terms of the Supreme Court's decision, there was no getting around the fact that Story's decision had articulated support for Southern claims upon the federal government to uphold slave law in the Northern states. The new personal liberty laws illustrated the increasing determination of the Northern populace to resist the slaveholder's hold over the federal government.

As Northern legislatures passed their personal liberty laws and as larger swathes of the Northern population showed a willingness to give aid to fugitives, Southerners began to demand a revision of the Fugitive Slave Law. Because state officials refused to aid in the process of rendition, they argued that there needed to be a greater federal presence in the North that would serve the slaveholder interest. In 1848 Senator Andrew P. Butler of South Carolina presented a bill that would provide for federal oversight over fugitive renditions. Nothing initially came of this proposal, but in January 1850 Senator James M. Mason of Virginia reintroduced the idea in Congress, and it began to take hold. What Butler, Mason, and their Southern supporters were promoting was the creation of a federal bureaucracy for slave-catching. Federal authority would be expanded in order to counter Northern state laws that were being used to interfere with slave claims.

This promotion of the expansion of federal power flew in the face of popular Southern arguments about slavery as a state issue. The idea that "states' rights" superseded federal power had gained a lot of traction in the South during the 1830s and 1840s after the so-called "Nullification Crisis."[14] Angry over the passage of federal tariff legislation that favored Northern manufacturing over Southern agricultural interests, South Carolina politicians led by John C. Calhoun had argued for the their right to nullify it—to make it "null and void" in South Carolina. In support of this action, they asserted that their state had the right to overturn federal laws that state lawmakers deemed unfair. The Constitution, they argued, had been a compact among the states, and the states had a right to revise or reject this compact if the federal government acted unconstitutionally. A threat of secession accompanied the South Carolina representatives' demands for the right of nullification. Leaders of the federal government, however, rejected the logic behind South Carolina's states' rights rhetoric. President Andrew Jackson threatened to use federal troops to enforce federal law in the state, and a bill was passed through Congress that would give him the right to do so. This angered many Southern leaders, but Senator Henry Clay helped to assuage their sense of grievance by introducing compromise legislation that had gradually lowered the tariff. The crisis was averted, but the doctrine of "states' rights" flourished in the South, especially concerning the place of slavery within the nation. Slavery was a state issue, Calhoun and other Southern leaders insisted, and the federal government thus had no authority over state policies concerning the institution.

Southern demands for a federally enforced fugitive slave law, however, revealed the extent to which the doctrine of states' rights was an argument of convenience. However loudly Southern leaders insisted upon their commitment to this ideology, they were not consistent in their promotion of it. When states' rights arguments served the interests of plantation owners and slaveholders, they were trotted out. When stronger federal action would help to strengthen their claims over their slaves, Southern slaveholders were all too willing to expand the oversight of the federal government in order to counter Northern expressions of their own states' rights to reject the claims of slaveholders.

• • •

Jerry had only recently arrived in Syracuse when Mason's bill to revise fugitive slave policy was introduced in Congress. The possibility of its passage struck fear in the hearts of free blacks throughout the North because it would make it more difficult to avoid the slave catcher. They would be more vulnerable under the new law, and many considered removing themselves to across the American border into Canada. Jerry must have considered this option, but he decided to remain in Syracuse.

Jerry's decision to remain was risky, for on the American side of the Canadian–United States border he was vulnerable to re-enslavement.

Nevertheless he chose to stay, for Syracuse had a well-established, if contested, reputation as an antislavery stronghold. Antislavery societies had appeared in western New York as the Northern state emancipations had taken place, and in the 1830s the abolition movement—the movement to end slavery unconditionally and immediately—took hold and grew. Some Syracuse residents considered abolitionists fanatical and dangerous to the American Union, but the membership of the abolitionist organizations rose over time, and by 1850 the movement had a strong presence in Syracuse and its vicinity. In addition, the small black community of Syracuse was active in promoting self-improvement and providing protection for its members. Especially encouraging to Jerry, Syracuse was well known for its Underground Railroad activity. Numerous fugitives had taken refuge in the city, and even more had been aided on their journey to the safety of British Canada. For all of these reasons, Jerry had reason to believe he was safe in the town.

But Jerry was not forgotten in Missouri. After lawmakers in Washington, DC, put into place Butler's proposed slave-catching bureaucracy in 1850, John McReynolds decided to purchase the slave who had seized his freedom. If he could find Jerry, by the terms of the new law the federal government would be bound to provide aid in detaining him and returning him to Missouri. McReynolds' gamble paid off, for Jerry's whereabouts were soon ascertained. A friend had been traveling in New York, and he recognized the red-headed slave in Syracuse. He sent word to Missouri with the news, and McReynolds quickly followed up. He dispatched his neighbor, James Lear, who was traveling to New York on business, to retrieve Jerry.[15] Under the provisions of the new law, Lear could approach a federal commissioner in Syracuse with proof of Jerry's slave status and McReynolds' ownership, demand that federal marshals aid in Jerry's detention, and, upon obtaining a certificate of rendition from the commissioner, quietly bring Jerry back to Missouri. Federal law would support their endeavor. Whether or not the law would be fulfilled in the antislavery stronghold of Syracuse, however, was in question.

CHAPTER 3

....

Union

Syracuse federal commissioner Joseph Sabine had ordered Jerry's arrest, and after Jerry was detained on October 1, he was in the unenviable position of deciding the man's fate. Sabine took his duties as a federal official seriously, but he was no fan of the law that required him to assist in the rendition of fugitive slaves. According to later reminiscences of his wife, Margaret, both she and her husband were "staunch abolitionists." Nevertheless, she said, her husband was also "a firm believer in obedience to the laws of his country."[1] Although Mrs. Sabine may have exaggerated both her own and her husband's abolitionist inclinations later in life, it is clear that Sabine was uncomfortable with his new duties under the Fugitive Slave Law of 1850, which had been passed several months after he was appointed to his office.[2] He was now called upon to execute the new law and thus faced a difficult choice: obey the law of the land and send a man into slavery, or turn his back on the law and preserve a man's freedom.

Sabine had hoped that the letter of the law would be on his side when James Lear approached him about detaining Jerry in early September 1851. Unconvinced by Lear's claim, Sabine demanded that he produce a deed of sale and proof of Jerry's identity before he would issue an arrest warrant. Lear did not have adequate documentation, and so he traveled to Cooperstown, New York, with the intention of gaining a warrant from a Judge Nelson, whom he was told would be more sympathetic to his case. He was disappointed to find that the judge was out of town until October 10. The slave owner's agent was thus forced to write to John McReynolds in Missouri, requesting the required papers. When McReynolds received this request, he dispatched a local sheriff, Samuel Smith, to New York with the materials. Only when Smith arrived in Syracuse on September 30, 1851 with the required documentation did Sabine agree to Jerry's arrest.[3]

While they waited for the papers from Missouri, Lear demanded that Syracuse authorities bring additional assistance to the city to help with the seizure of the runaway. According to the new Fugitive Slave Law of 1850, this was his right. Syracuse federal marshal Henry W. Allen therefore summoned fellow marshals from the towns of Auburn, Canandaigua, and Rochester to Syracuse to render any necessary aid. They arrived in late September and awaited further instructions. Allen also enlisted the assistance of members of the local police force.[4]

When the requested documentation arrived from Missouri, Sabine was forced into action. According to law he must bring Jerry in and hold a hearing. Margaret Sabine recalled how distressed her husband had been when he told her about the situation. He was bound to perform his duty as federal commissioner, but he did not want to condemn a man to a lifetime of slavery. "It is cowardly to resign before my first case comes to trial," he said to her, "but what else can I do?"

Margaret had responded, "Hold on to your commission, let no other man have your place." She argued that Sabine could do more to help the fugitive if he maintained his office than if he gave it up to some less conscientious person. She expressed confidence that justice would somehow win out. Sabine heeded his wife's advice and hoped for the best. The events surrounding Jerry's arrest, however, would cause him to resign his position within just a few weeks.[5]

Although sharpened by his official role, Sabine's dilemma mirrored that which Northerners with antislavery views faced under the terms of the new Fugitive Slave Law, passed in September 1850. It presented them with a choice between adherence to their own consciences and obedience to American law. Some argued that the law must be respected, while others insisted that it must be defied. Most, however, were like Joseph Sabine, bewildered by the choice they must make. In their view it was not just respect for the law that was at stake. It was also about the fate of the American Union, for the Fugitive Slave Law of 1850 was part of a compromise that was meant to end yet another sectional crisis over the expansion of slavery into new territories. Such an inflammatory law would never have been passed if it had not been intertwined with the deeper concern for the Union. Many Northerners, even some who had no concern about the morality of slavery, felt that it gave unjustified power to the federal government in a matter that was assumed to be under state jurisdiction. For the sake of national unity, however, some individuals who believed that the law was immoral and, perhaps, unconstitutional, argued that it nevertheless must be obeyed.

• • •

At the center of the fears for Union in 1850 was the land ceded from Mexico in 1848 under the Treaty of Guadalupe Hidalgo. That treaty had ended the U.S.–Mexican War and given the United States possession of the northern third of Mexico, an area that encompassed what would become the state of California and the territories of New Mexico and Utah. The settlement with Mexico sparked a burst of nationalist spirit in the young republic as the United States became a continental nation, but within that spirit laid seeds of sectional discord.

The issue was the same one that had emerged during the Missouri Crisis. Would slavery be legal or illegal in the nation's new lands? Compromise, however, was a more difficult proposition in 1850 due to the presence of other sectional questions regarding slavery, like the institution's existence in the nation's capital and the enforcement of the Fugitive Slave Law. In addition, since 1830 antislavery activity had grown in the North, provoking defensiveness in the South about slaveholding. Southerners had become more aggressive in promoting their "Southern rights," and this had, in turn, increased the sense throughout the North that the "slave power" was dominating American politics and that Southern leaders needed to be put in their place. Political leaders looked for a way to quell the sectional tensions.

Kentucky Whig Senator Henry Clay had been instrumental in helping to broker compromises on issues that caused friction between the North and the South in the decades before the U.S.–Mexican War. In his previous position as Speaker of the House he had promoted the congressional compromise that had averted the crisis over

Henry Clay.
Print Collection, Miriam and Ira D. Wallach Division of Art, Prints and Photographs, The New York Public Library, Astor, Lenox and Tilden Foundations

Missouri statehood in 1820, and a decade later he had worked to quell the tensions produced by the Nullification Crisis. By 1850, Clay's reputation as "the Great Compromiser" had been cemented. It seemed appropriate that he would construct a compromise proposal to deal with the conflict that had grown out of the U.S.–Mexican War.[6] Ironically, part of his compromise would include the passage of the Fugitive Slave Law of 1850, which would stimulate throughout the North echoes of the rhetoric of nullification that earlier had emanated from the South.

The question of what to do with lands gained in the Mexican conquest was addressed in Congress before the war was even won. In August 1846, a young Democratic member of the House of Representatives, David Wilmot, proposed an amendment to a bill for funding the war that would disallow involuntary servitude in the lands the United States acquired from Mexico. This amendment became known as the Wilmot Proviso. Charting a similar course as the Tallmadge Amendment had a quarter of a century before, the proviso passed through the House of Representatives, which had a Northern majority, but it failed in the Senate, where Southern interests held sway. After the failure in the Senate, the proviso was reintroduced repeatedly in the House, only to be voted down again and again in the Senate. The act of a Northern congressman had once again made the issue of slavery in the territories one of the nation's foremost political issues.

After the war was won, Americans elected Whig war hero Zachary Taylor to the presidency, charging him with the responsibility of leading the nation through the controversy that the war had sparked. Taylor believed that the speedy admission of all the territories would alleviate the sectional tensions. He pressed that California should immediately be admitted to the Union as a state. He also urged that New Mexico and Utah organize as territories and apply for statehood as quickly as possible. Slavery had been illegal in these territories under Mexican law, and so he presumed that they would come in as free states.

Southern congressmen vigorously opposed both the Wilmot Proviso and the president's proposal. They argued that any circumscription of slavery in the new lands would erect a barrier to the expansion of slavery and violate Southerners' property rights. Southern leaders banded together, and a call was made for Southern delegates to meet in Nashville, Tennessee to discuss the protection of Southern interests. Some from the South began to speak of secession from the United States if the federal government did not support the right to hold human property in the new territories.

Debates over how the federal government should organize the new Mexican territories absorbed the American people after 1848, but other issues also contributed to the sectional political tensions. For one, Northern petitioners were demanding an end to both the slave trade and slavery in Washington, DC. Congress had no authority to legislate on slavery in the states, but it did have jurisdiction over the nation's capital, and those with an antislavery bent were increasingly disgusted with the display of slave sales and slave labor in the seat of the republic. On the other side of the sectional divide, Southern leaders complained of the lack of enforcement in the North of the constitutionally sanctioned Fugitive Slave Law of 1793, and they were making demands for the institution of a slave-catching bureaucracy with a revised Fugitive Slave Law. Many Northerners vehemently opposed this Southern demand, viewing the proposed measure as a draconian one that not only violated the rights of Northern blacks but also those of white residents. It gave too much power to the federal government and made requirements of Northern citizens that, they believed, clearly violated their state laws concerning slavery.

The question of the expansion of slavery into new territories merged together with these other issues, and in 1850 the nation experienced a full blown sectional crisis—one that many felt seriously endangered the Union. The 31st Congress thus would have its work cut out for it when it convened in Washington, DC, to sort out these issues.

Henry Clay hoped to avert the sense of crisis with a compromise that would settle the sectional division over slavery once and for all. In January 1850, he presented a series of resolutions in the Senate that together, he hoped, would provide "an amicable arrangement of all questions between the free and slave states, growing out of the subject of slavery." He proposed that California be admitted to the Union as soon as possible. California had already made a Constitution outlawing slavery, and it would thus enter as a free state. The rest of the territories, he suggested, should be organized quickly and the people of those territories themselves should decide upon the question of slavery. Clay felt that geographical and climate considerations would prevent slavery from taking root in these areas, and so there was little need for Congress to impose any kind of restrictions. In dealing with the territory of New Mexico, Clay included in his proposal measures that would settle a boundary dispute between the new territory and the slave-owning state of Texas. Clay also recommended that slavery should not be abolished in Washington, DC, but that the slave trade should end in the nation's capital, as it was an "abomination." And, in order to appease the South, which would most likely see no territorial gains for slavery under his plan, Clay backed the new Fugitive Slave Bill.[7]

After he presented the compromise package, Clay noted that it required representatives of both the North and the South to make concessions. If he had asked more of the North than the South, he said, it was because he believed that less was at stake for Northerners

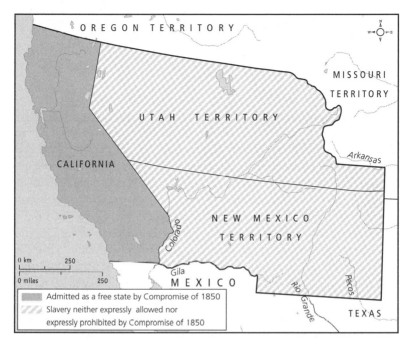

Territory gained by the United States in the U.S.–Mexican War.
Map by Alliance USA

concerning slavery. Comparing Northern attacks on slavery to the Southern defense of the institution, Clay said that in the North "we behold sentiment, sentiment, sentiment alone," but in the South what was at stake was "property, the social fabric, life, and all that makes life desirable and happy."[8] On February 5, he made an address to the Senate calling on American lawmakers to support the compromise in order to avert disunion—to "pause at the edge of the precipice, before the fearful and disastrous leap is taken into the yawning abyss below."[9]

Clay's plea immediately gave focus to the sectional debates in Congress, and new alignments took shape, complicating the dynamics of the American party system. Instead of the traditional contest between two political parties, Congress was now divided according to opinion on the compromise. Unionist elements within both the Whig and Democratic parties and from both the North and South praised Clay's plan as a viable way to end the sectional tensions in the nation. Ultras on both sides of the slavery issue, however, were angered at the provisions that asked them to give way.

• • •

The sectional debates in Congress extended outward from Washington, DC. In the South, newspapers and Southern spokesmen clamored for their right to take their slaves where they pleased within the Union. Throughout the North, the opening of new territories to the possibility of slave-owning was hotly contested, and many Northerners saw the new Fugitive Slave Bill as an anathema. In Syracuse, as in other Northern cities, antislavery elements organized conventions and petition drives to weigh in on the territorial question as well as on other issues concerning slavery. And in Syracuse, as in other Northern cities, these efforts were starting to attract a broader array of Northern citizens who were increasingly critical of slavery as sectional issues invaded politics. As more Northerners began to speak out against Southern slavery, this led others to question the impact that this sentiment would have on the Union. It also led to an intensification of debates within the antislavery movement about the best way to respond to sectional political issues.

CHAPTER 4

....

Abolitionists

When Gerrit Smith arrived at Commissioner Sabine's office to find twenty-one marshals and deputies guarding the handcuffed and much distressed Jerry, he immediately told the prisoner that he would defend him "at any expense" and "leave no stone unturned" to secure his freedom. He was one of the richest men in the nation, and he told Jerry that he would support him with his fortune. In his autobiography, fellow Liberty Party man Jermain Loguen recalled that with Smith's promise "the countenance of Jerry brightened," for "what fugitive slave, if he has been in the country a short time, has not heard of Gerrit Smith? Or sitting by his side, is not inspired by the aura that surrounds him?" As the people of Syracuse crowded into Commissioner Sabine's office and down the hallway, Jerry turned to Smith:

> "I believe," said Jerry, "if I should throw myself upon this crowd, they would help me to escape—they look like friends."
>
> "They are friends," said Mr. Smith, "but not yet. I mean you shall escape—but not yet."[1]

From the moment of the arrest, Smith would be a key player in the defense of both Jerry's rights and of the rights of Syracuse citizens who wished to aid the former slave. His involvement was expected by everyone, for Smith was usually at the center of abolitionist activities in upstate New York.

• • •

$200 Reward

Left the service of the subscriber on the evening

of the 7th inst. a Bright Quadroon Servant-girl, about twenty-four years of age, named HARRIET. Said girl was about 5 feet high, of a full and well proportioned form, straight light brown hair, dark eyes, approaching to black, of fresh complexion, and so fair that she would generally be taken for white; a prominent mouth with depressed nostrils and receding forehead, readily betrayed to the critical observer the leading traits of the African race. Her demeanor is very quiet, and her deportment modest.

At the time of leaving she had on a black dress of figured poplin. She took with her one green Merino dress; one pink Gingham (checked) do.; one French Muslin figured do.; one Buff, and one light purple Calico do. She wore small rings (with stones) in her ears, and had three chased Gold Rings on her fingers, two of which were set with green and the other with transparent chrystal. She also took with her a plaid blanket Shawl, but left her bonnet, so that her head-dress cannot be described.

In leaving the service of the subscriber, she leaves her aged mother and a younger sister, who are devotedly attached to her, and to whom she has ever appeared much attached. It may be proper also to state, that her conduct as a servant, and her moral deportment so far as the same have come to the knowledge of the subscriber, have hitherto been irreproachable. It is believed that she has been spirited away from the service of the undersigned, by the officious and persevering efforts of certain malicious and designing persons, operating through the agency of the colored people of Syracuse, at which place he had been induced to spend a few days. The subscriber would further add, that he has refused several importunate offers of $2,500 for said girl, for the sole reason that he would never consent to part her from the other members of her family, and it is chiefly with the hope of restoring her to her aged mother and sister, who will be plunged in sorrow at the separation, that this notice is published. The above reward of Two Hundred Dollars will be paid to any person who will deliver said girl to the proprietor Syracuse House, in Syracuse, or one hun___ed D_____ anyone who will give such information as shall lead to her

___se, October 9th, _____ J. DAVENPORT

Reward poster for Harriet Powell, posted in Syracuse in 1839.
From the Collection of the Onondaga Historical Association, 321 Montgomery Street, Syracuse, NY 13202

Smith, in fact, had already played a prominent role in an earlier slave rescue that took place in Syracuse a little over a decade before Jerry was arrested. He had participated in the liberation of the young and beautiful Harriet Powell, an event that had helped to shape the anti-slavery reputation of Syracuse, and, indeed, had encouraged Jerry to feel that he was safe in that town.[2]

On October 9, 1839 there had appeared a handbill in Syracuse offering a $200 reward for the capture of a "Bright Quadroon Servant-Girl." The handbill begged those with any knowledge of her whereabouts to bring her back to her owner, John Davenport. It did not describe Harriet as a fugitive, but instead asserted that she was a woman "seduced" or "spirited away" by "malicious and designing persons, operating through the agency of the colored people of Syracuse." The handbill announced that Davenport had turned down offers of $2500 for the girl in the past "for the sole reason that he would never consent to part her from the other members of her family," and it explained that it was "chiefly with the hope of restoring her to her aged mother and sister" that he sought her return. It was a model of the paternalistic language often employed by slave owners who asserted that their only wish was to take care of their slaves, but it also indicated the real reason for the Davenport's wish for her return—Harriet's significant value as human property.[3]

The Davenports were Mississippi planters who were residing in the Syracuse House hotel while visiting relatives who lived nearby, and they had brought Harriet with them to tend to their children during the visit. Jermain Loguen, who wrote in his autobiography not only of the events surrounding the arrest of Jerry but also of this earlier defiance of fugitive slave law, described the family's arrival in Syracuse, noting that Davenport and his wife traveled with "another white lady who was finely dressed." When Syracuse residents realized that this "other white lady" was a slave, Loguen said, "the fact that a woman so white and attractive was held as property awakened curiosity and indignation among some who had no objection to black slavery."[4]

African American residents of the city also took an interest in the Davenports' slave. Many of the workers at Syracuse House were members of the town's black community, and they felt sympathy for Harriet. In particular, Thomas Leonard, a thirty-eight-year-old waiter and coachmen who was himself a fugitive from Virginia, sought to render aid. Soon after her arrival, Leonard approached Harriet and offered to help her gain her freedom. He explained that there were people in Syracuse who could help her to escape to Canada, beyond the reach of her owners. Harriet was reluctant to take the risk, but Leonard convinced her that she would be safe. Once she agreed to a plan of escape, Leonard, along with other black hotel employees, enlisted the aid of several white citizens— William C. Clarke, who was the deputy county clerk of Syracuse, and John B. Owen, a marble dealer. Both were abolitionists, and they were eager to render aid. Together they all arranged for Harriet's escape.

The escape took place on October 8, the day that the Davenports planned to leave New York. A party was held in order to bid them farewell at the home of Major William A. Cook. The night of the party was dark, a good one for flight, and the plans for Harriet's escape were carried off without a hitch. Harriet, who attended the party to care for the Davenports' child, brought the infant that was her charge to Mrs. Davenport, asking to take a short break. She then walked out the back door where she met a contact who walked her to a waiting carriage. Leonard showed up with clothes that he had procured from her room, and the carriage rushed her down Onondaga Street all the way to the village of Marcellus, where she would take temporary refuge.

When Harriet failed to reappear at the party, the host immediately suspended the affair, an alarm was sounded, and Syracuse city leaders sent scouts out in all directions looking for the young woman. They searched the homes of all the abolitionists in town. Men also searched prominent abolitionist households in nearby areas, including Gerrit Smith's house in Peterboro. City officials arrested Leonard and charged him with stealing clothing from the Davenports, hoping that this would pressure him into revealing Harriet's whereabouts. He gave nothing away and eventually was released.

They did not find Harriet. "The white and black men managed this enterprise so prudently and bravely," Loguen explained in his account of the affair, "that no trace of the one or the other could be scented by the bloodhounds." There was, however, one close call. Rumors spread about Harriet's whereabouts in Marcellus, and information leaked out to men who wished to claim the reward for her return. Luckily, the abolitionists of Syracuse learned of their plans to travel to Marcellus before they could be carried out. They held a meeting at the Congregational Church, where they collected donations in order to "ship a bale of Southern goods."[5]

It was at this meeting that Gerrit Smith became involved. The funds raised at the meeting were handed over to Smith, who instructed Harriet's guardians to get the young woman to his estate in Peterboro, about twenty-five miles southeast of Syracuse. Clarke and Owen made arrangements to move Harriet to Smith's place, and after a few stops on the way, she arrived at the philanthropist's home.

Elizabeth Cady Stanton, who would later gain fame as an abolitionist and one of the founders of the women's rights movement, wrote of her memories of meeting Harriet at her cousin Gerrit's house when she was twenty-four years old. She was at Smith's residence in October 1839 when he invited her up to the third story of his house. There she was introduced to Harriet. According to

Stanton, Smith said to the young fugitive, "Harriet, I have brought all my young cousins to see you. I want you to make good abolitionists of them by telling them the history of your life—what you have seen and suffered in slavery." Harriet spoke for two hours about her experiences, and then later that night Elizabeth and her other cousins helped to prepare Harriet for a carriage ride North toward her final destination in Canada. According to Stanton, they all wept as they heard Harriet's story. "We needed no further education to make us earnest abolitionists," she said.[6]

After a short stay at Smith's residence, Harriet was transported to the Canadian town of Kingston, just across the border. Due to the efforts of black and white agents in Syracuse, as well as her own willingness to risk flight, Harriet would live out the rest of her life as a free woman. She would marry, and her children would be born into freedom.

The details of Harriet's escape shed light on why Jerry took refuge in Syracuse in 1850. The town was at the center of an active Underground Railroad network in central New York. Although not all of its residents supported this network's challenge to the legitimacy of slavery, those who did were willing to go to great lengths to promote, and protect, liberty for those claimed as slaves.

• • •

Gerrit Smith was a key member of this network, but he had not been born into an antislavery household. In fact, like many wealthy New Yorkers of his time, his father had owned slaves. Peter Smith had been in the fur trade with John Jacob Astor in upstate New York at the end of the previous century and had invested a large portion of his profits from the trade in land, accumulating hundreds of thousands of acres throughout New York and some holdings in other states. As a young man, Gerrit took control of the family business, and from his estate in Peterboro—the hamlet that bore the first name of his father—he managed the family's vast wealth and land holdings. Although later in life he would claim that he had seen early on that "slave holding was egregiously wrong," there is little evidence in Smith's youth to predict the extent of his later work on the slave's behalf.[7]

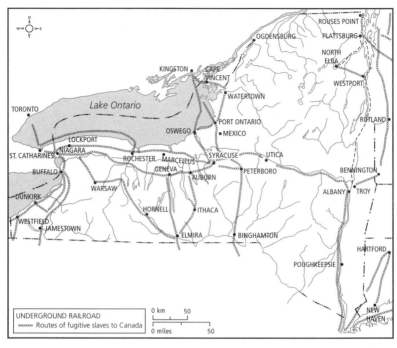

New York Underground Railroad routes. Map adapted from a rendering by
W. H. Siebert, 1898.
Map by Alliance USA

Smith was not raised in a particularly religious household, but
after he came of age he was greatly affected by the evangelical revivals
of the Second Great Awakening that swept through the nation during
the 1820s and 1830s. During those decades, preachers and church lay
leaders of various Protestant denominations responded to the growing secularism, materialism, and corruption they saw in nineteenth
century American society with sermons and revivals aimed at rein-
vigorating religious feeling. Central to this wave of revivalism was a
belief in the perfectibility of mankind. Evangelical leaders emphasized that individuals had it within their power to make both themselves and the larger social order within which they lived perfect in
God's eyes. They thus emphasized the importance of improving

society as well as one's self and encouraged active involvement in social reform movements.

Revivalism was especially strong in the towns along the recently constructed Erie Canal that connected New York City to the western states. The canal, finished in 1825, opened up the New York frontier to ministers who spread their message in the young communities, like Syracuse and Peterboro, that grew on or near the new transportation artery. Revival meetings took place frequently throughout the emerging region, and western New York became known as the "Burned-Over District" because the evangelical fires of the Awakening had so overtaken the area. Smith was situated in the middle of these fires, and he embraced their message of Christian perfectionism and reform.[8]

Smith's evangelical awakening led him to the decision to use his wealth to help others. He bankrolled many institutions and reform organizations, and he provided relief to individuals in need. Among the many causes he embraced were educational reform, dress reform, poor relief, temperance, anti-tobacco campaigns, vegetarianism, the establishment of domestic and foreign missions, women's rights, and, most importantly, the movement to end slavery.

Smith's interest in antislavery and black uplift led him first to the colonization movement. In the 1820s and early 1830s he was a supporter of the American Colonization Society (ACS), an organization founded in 1816 that encouraged the migration of free blacks to Africa. Smith embraced this goal as a way to encourage emancipation, promote black uplift, and to bring ideals about democracy and Christianity to Africa. He was particularly interested in the missionary aspect of the project. The ACS had established a colony on the west coast of Africa called Liberia. ACS proponents argued that Liberia would serve as a place where African Americans, once removed from North America, could create a black republic modeled on the United States. From there, they could spread Christianity and democracy into surrounding areas. Smith applauded these objectives, and he contributed around $10,000 to the ACS during the time he was associated with the movement.[9]

But colonization soon came under attack. Many free blacks viewed the movement not as a humanitarian endeavor but instead as a racist effort to remove black people from white society. Most leaders of the black community insisted that they had no wish to go to the African colony of Liberia, which was as foreign to them as it was to white Americans. The United States was their home. They had helped to build the young republic, and they insisted that true reform would promote equality between whites and blacks within the United States, so that all of its inhabitants could enjoy the fruits of their own labor.

These criticisms from members of the Northern black community eventually caught the attention of some antislavery-oriented white Americans. Up until the 1830s most white reformers who agitated against slavery supported colonization and advocated a gradual end to slavery in the South, similar to that which had recently taken place throughout the North. Now, under the influence of the perfectionist spirit of the Great Awakening, they were moved by demands for justice that emanated from the free black communities that had been produced by the Northern emancipations. The abolition movement was born as these reformers moved away from the promotion of colonization and gradual emancipation and allied with black leaders in the call for the immediate, unconditional abolition of slavery in the South and for uplift and equality for African Americans throughout the United States. William Lloyd Garrison, himself a convert from colonization, became the acknowledged leader of this movement. Headquartered in Boston, he published an antislavery newspaper, the *Liberator*, and along with distinguished New Yorkers Arthur and Lewis Tappan and black abolitionists like Robert Purvis of Philadelphia, he established the American Anti-Slavery Society (AASS) in 1833.[10]

The members of the AASS mobilized in order to persuade fellow Americans that slavery needed to be abolished unconditionally and immediately. They circulated antislavery literature throughout the North and mailed it to slave owners in the South in an effort at "moral suasion." Itinerant speakers traveled throughout the free states promoting the cause and encouraging the establishment of local and state antislavery societies. White leaders of the movement reached out to African Americans, especially former slaves like the famous Frederick Douglass, to serve as lecturers. They understood that exposure to black voices would help to humanize the slavery issue among whites, who too often debated slavery in abstract, political terms. By the end of the 1830s an energetic biracial movement for the abolition of slavery and for black equality had emerged in the Northern states.

As the abolition movement grew, its members lured Gerrit Smith away from colonization. As with many converts, it was initially the persecution that the abolitionists faced that sparked Smith's interest in their movement. A turning point for Smith was a meeting in Utica, New York, in the fall of 1835. Abolition leaders from around the state had planned a convention in order to unite local antislavery organizations into a state abolition society. Smith attended the abolitionist's convention mainly out of curiosity, but the events surrounding it would pull him into their movement.

When abolitionists from around the state of New York—between four and six hundred of them—arrived at the Second Presbyterian Church in Utica on October 21, 1835, an anti-abolitionist mob arose in protest of their convention. Town leaders feared violence and urged the abolitionists to disband for the sake of order. Smith responded to the situation with an invitation to the attendees to repair for the evening in Peterboro. They could gather at his estate where he would arrange for their stay with nearby residents, and they could reconvene the next day. Many of them accepted Smith's offer and made the thirty mile journey southwest, traveling first along the Erie Canal, and then over land to Smith's home. The next day, on October 22, they resumed their meeting at Peterboro's Presbyterian Church, where they successfully formed the New York Anti-Slavery Society (NYASS).

Smith, now cast in the role of host, spoke out at this meeting in support of the abolitionists' efforts. He was especially concerned with asserting their right to assemble and to free speech. "The enormous and insolent demands of the South, sustained, I am deeply ashamed to say, by craven and mercenary spirits at the North, manifest beyond all dispute, that the question now is not merely, nor mainly, whether the blacks of the South shall remain slaves," he said, "but whether the whites at the North shall become slaves also."[11] Smith eventually joined and assumed a leadership role over the NYASS, stating that one of the key reasons he shifted his support to the abolitionist organization was because the "Society is now so far identified with the right of free discussion . . . that if the Society be suffered to fall, the right of free discussion will fall with it."[12] One of the most important duties of antislavery reformers was to "publish the truth about slavery," he believed, and this could not be done if the right of free speech was not respected in the North.[13]

Historian Gerald Sorin has pointed out how Smith's conversion to the abolition movement fit into a general pattern leading to its spread in the Northern states. "Whites who wavered on the question of abolition," he wrote, "could be drawn to the support of immediatism if they became convinced that the long arm of slavery was reaching into their personal lives, whether by mob action, economic threat, free speech and free assembly, opposition in churches, or denial of the right to petition the government."[14] Smith was converted to the movement because of his concern with the right of free speech, and from there his commitment would grow. Other abolitionists, in New York and beyond, experienced similar conversions.

The circumscription of white rights led many to the movement against slavery, and from there some reformers progressed to an

Gerrit Smith.
From the Collection of the Madison County Historical Society, Oneida, NY

overarching concern for universal rights. Those, like Smith, who made this progression became abolitionists who promoted the immediate, unconditional emancipation of the slave. Others remained primarily concerned with the way in which the system of slavery corrupted guarantees of liberty and opportunity for whites. They were committed to a more limited antislavery vision, advocating colonization, gradual emancipation, or limits to the expansion of slavery beyond the states where it already existed.

· · ·

In addition to his involvement with the NYASS, Smith would for a short time become a member of the American Anti-Slavery Society (AASS). During the late 1830s Smith provided financial and moral support for the central organization, but the focus of his own action remained in New York, and indeed much of the antislavery activity of western New York gravitated around Smith. While Smith initially cooperated with the AASS and Garrison's "Boston clique" of abolitionists, over time the bond between Smith and Garrison would break over the question of "means": the best way to bring about change. Garrison insisted that the abolition movement must rely primarily on moral suasion and not corrupt itself with involvement in party politics, while Smith became an advocate of political abolitionism. The views of each man would dominate their respective regions. In the 1840s, New England remained the center of "Garrisonian" abolitionism while political abolitionism flourished in upstate New York.

This division was part of a larger rift that took place among abolitionists as the movement matured. During the 1830s the abolitionists were hopeful that they would be able to use moral suasion to convince Southern slave-owners to emancipate their slaves and to promote racial justice in both the North and South. As the decade wore on, it became evident that their hopes would not be fulfilled. The leaders of Southern states refused to deliver abolitionist literature through the mails, a "gag rule" was instituted in Congress forbidding the discussion of antislavery petitions, those suspected of abolitionist views were persecuted in both the North and South, and Southerners developed more aggressive pro-slavery arguments defending their way of life. Instead of a turn toward emancipation, the abolitionists were confronted with a more stringent pro-slavery South and with an anti-abolitionist backlash in the North. Thus, many began to question the methods of their movement.

The disagreement between Smith and Garrison was about political action, but other issues were also involved in the fragmenting of the abolition movement. One of the most contested issues was the role that women should play in the AASS. While Garrison supported a strong, active role for women, other more conservative abolitionists, like the Tappan brothers of New York City, thought it was improper for women to be so involved in the public sphere. Many of these men were evangelicals who also worried about what they believed to be Garrison's general attack on religion. As he had done with political parties, Garrison advised abolitionists to reject the established churches in the nation because they too had compromised with slaveholders in order to maintain unity. Finally, some abolitionists worried that Garrison was merging his support for too many other causes—like pacifism, anti-Sabbatarianism, and women's rights—with the antislavery movement.

For his part, Smith held many of the same views on the corruption of American institutions as Garrison, and their points of view were not that far apart. Smith felt that women should take a strong role in the movement, and, like Garrison, he considered his abolitionism to be part of a more generalized effort to purify society. Smith also worried about the corruption of both the established churches and the political parties. Unlike Garrison, however, Smith did not reject the general idea of religious or political institutional involvement. Instead he sought to replace old, corrupt organizations with new, virtuous ones. When he felt that the Presbyterian Church he attended had become complicit with slavery, he left and formed a new "Free Church" in Peterboro that supported abolition. As he became disgusted with both the Whig and the Democratic Parties for their unwillingness to stand united against slavery, he was instrumental in the formation a new antislavery political party—the Liberty Party.

Smith's interest in political action had begun shortly after he joined the abolition movement. In 1837, as president of the NYASS, he advocated that members refrain from voting for any candidate that did not condemn slavery. Under his leadership, the society developed a questionnaire for political candidates that would serve as a litmus test for their stance on the subject. Because an antislavery position was politically detrimental in the late 1830s, few candidates passed, and so members of the NYASS found themselves voluntarily disenfranchised. Frustrated by this situation, Smith and many other New York abolitionists met at a convention in Oswego, New York in 1839 to form an antislavery third party that would run its own slate of antislavery candidates. Although they had little chance of winning any major elections, they could influence politics by holding the balance of power between the Whig and the Democratic Parties in some locales. Smith believed that the primary role of government was to protect the natural rights of all men and women and that God's laws should be the basis of all human laws. His goal for the Liberty Party was to establish a third party that would conform to this view of government, and he hoped that it would be an instrument in reforming the American political system.

When Smith and his New York colleagues formed the Liberty Party, they split from the AASS. Garrison was critical of the political abolitionists' willingness to involve themselves in party politics, which, he believed, would endanger their own purity of thought. The fundamental disagreement that sprung up between the AASS and the Liberty Party during the 1840s, though, lay in their differing views of the American Union and its Constitution. The Liberty Party asserted that the preservation of the American Union was important and that it could be legally purged of slavery because they saw the Constitution as fundamentally an antislavery document. Garrison and his supporters argued that the Constitution upheld slavery, and eventually Garrison would advocate a separation of the Northern states from the slaveholding South.

• • •

During the 1840s, upstate New York became a bastion of political abolitionism, and the town of Syracuse became a center of Liberty Party activity. Smith made frequent visits to the neighboring town from Peterboro. Many Syracuse residents became members of the party, and the city hosted many of its meetings and conventions. Not all of the residents of Syracuse were abolitionists, and not all of the abolitionists were Liberty Party members; but because of the presence of the political abolitionists, the question of federal complicity in slavery was kept before the town's eyes throughout that decade. Federal policy concerning slavery would become of even greater concern as sectional debates over the expansion of slavery into new territories and over federal fugitive slave policy heated up in the last half of the 1840s. The debates held in Washington over the nature of slavery and its place the American Union would reverberate throughout the American nation and would absorb the abolitionists of Syracuse.

CHAPTER 5

....

Syracuse

Samuel J. May was eating lunch at his Syracuse home on October 1, 1851, when he heard the church bells that signaled a fugitive's arrest. He quickly left his house to travel to a meeting place pre-arranged by the Vigilance Committee, almost a mile away. As he made his way to lend aid, he encountered other Syracuse residents who informed him that federal marshals had taken Jerry to the office of Federal Commissioner Sabine. May changed his course, heading directly to Sabine's office, where he joined the Liberty Party men who had come from the Congregational Church. When May arrived, the hearing, which he described as a "one-sided process" in which only Lear's claim on behalf of Jerry's owner would be needed to return Jerry to slavery, was already underway.[1]

Like Gerrit Smith and the Liberty Party men, May saw Jerry's arrest as a test case for federal fugitive slave policy, and he was deter-mined that the town of Syracuse would stand against it. Although May was associated with the Garrisonian abolitionists and not the Liberty Party, he often collaborated with Gerrit Smith and, like the Peterboro philanthropist, was one of the key figures of the New York abolition movement. The arrest of Jerry would force the two men even closer together as they became allies in the attempt to preserve the fugitive's freedom and to express their disdain for the Fugitive Slave Law. At the same time, differences of opinion about how to ad-dress the sectional issues that were the backdrop of that arrest would also highlight the divisions that existed among Northerners who, in growing numbers, opposed the institution of slavery.

• • •

Samuel J. May.
From the Collection of the Onondaga Historical Association, 321 Montgomery Street,
Syracuse, NY 13202

May, a Unitarian minister with Boston origins, had arrived in Syracuse in 1845 to lead the town's Unitarian church, the Church of the Messiah. By the time he arrived in New York, he was already an established abolitionist. In 1819, as a young man, he had attended a meeting protesting the Missouri Compromise in Boston. At it, a young Daniel Webster spoke against slavery and the slave trade. May came away with a reverence for Webster and a commitment to the battle against slavery in the United States. Like most white antislavery reformers of the time, May became involved with the colonization movement in the 1820s, and he helped to establish an auxiliary of the American Colonization Society in Connecticut. In 1830, however, he was exposed to the Garrisonian critique of colonization, and this inspired the then thirty-three-year old May to become an abolitionist. May was present at the formation of the American Anti-Slavery Society, and for the rest of his life he would remain a close ally of William Lloyd Garrison, whom he believed to be a "prophet" destined to bring moral change to American society. Even after he moved from New England to upstate New York in the 1840s, where political abolitionism held sway, May remained a committed Garrisonian. He would, however, not always agree with Garrison's tactics.[2]

Like both Garrison and Smith, May was involved in multiple reform movements aimed at perfecting American society. Particularly important to May were the peace movement and educational reform. Unlike his colleagues, however, his commitments grew not out of the evangelical fires of the Great Awakening but instead out of his commitment to the "Liberal Christianity" of the Unitarian Church. The Unitarians were an offshoot of the Congregational Church that had evolved out of the Puritan establishment in New England, and they sought to apply Enlightenment ideals and rationalism to religious doctrine. Unitarians viewed Jesus Christ not as divine but instead as an important prophet who was, explained May, "led by the Spirit of God, more constantly and entirely than any other son of man."[3] May's commitment to Unitarianism led him into both the ministry and the burgeoning reform movements of the antebellum period. Like other reformers, May sought to promote a perfect society. His vision of such a society, defined by his Unitarian beliefs, was not that different than the vision of Smith and other evangelicals. A perfect society was one that strove to live up to the biblical example of Christ and one that recognized natural rights, endowed by God, for all of mankind.

Although there was initial resistance in Syracuse to abolitionism during the early 1830s, May was optimistic about promoting reform in the city when he arrived. He had visited Syracuse several times previously, and he noted that during his stays he had "found quite a number of individuals . . . who had accepted the doctrines of the Immediate Abolitionists." A spirit of reform permeated Syracuse, and May credited its spread to other prominent antislavery lecturers who had visited the town, including Garrison, Smith, and Douglass. These men had "convinced . . . many people of the justice of their demands for the enslaved, and of the disastrous influence of the 'peculiar institution' of our Southern states." By the time he moved there, May said, "The community had come to respect somewhat the right of any who pleased to hold antislavery meetings."[4]

This respect was hard-won. Jermain Loguen writes of Syracuse in the 1830s: "There as in all the country, the churches and political parties were adapted to slavery as it was, and were unwilling to be disturbed by it. Indeed it was the judgment of those bodies that the prosperity of both Church and State demanded that the old state of things be undisturbed."⁵ Abolition thus took some time to take hold in the city. In 1835 when Syracuse town leaders learned of the plan to form a state antislavery society in Utica—the meeting that would ultimately take place in Peterboro at the behest of Gerrit Smith—they issued a public pronouncement against the abolitionists in the town newspaper stating that persons "who are known as Abolitionists or the friends of immediate emancipation . . . ought to be discountenanced as offenders against the public peace."⁶

The same year, when residents of Syracuse and the surrounding area planned a meeting at the town's Baptist Church in order to form the Onondaga County Anti-Slavery Society, there had been much resistance to the emergence of a local abolitionist organization. Anti-abolitionist crowds pelted those who showed up to attend the meeting with eggs and verbally abused the would-be society members. Gerrit Smith, visiting from Peterboro, was among those who were harassed. Anti-abolitionists also crashed the meeting and attempted to interfere with the formation of the new abolition society. The anti-abolitionist faction was not large enough to outvote the abolitionists, but the commotion they caused did succeed in preventing an orderly meeting from taking place. The uproar forced the Onondaga County abolitionists to adjourn. The next day, the antislavery men secretly reconvened ten miles to the east of Syracuse in the town of Fayetteville, where they succeeded in establishing their local society.⁷

Abolitionism also led to the fracturing of several churches in Syracuse. Both the Presbyterian and the Methodist churches split as a result of differing opinions on the movement. As evangelical revivals promoted an antislavery spirit among many congregants in the town, conservative ministers and church members bristled at what they saw as a radical movement that might alienate pro-slavery members of the church and thus threaten church unity. Some ministers spoke out against involvement in the antislavery movement, causing abolitionists in their congregations to leave their churches and form new ones that embraced the spirit of reform. After the mass exodus of reformers from the Presbyterian and Methodist churches in Syracuse, ministers of other congregations, fearing schism, avoided addressing the slavery issue altogether. May called the conservatism that existed among ministers of the established churches "the most serious obstacle to the progress of the anti-slavery cause." The problem, according to May, was that "the shepherds were driven by the sheep."[8]

By the late 1840s, however, out of twenty-five churches in Syracuse, there were five that were solidly antislavery: the Wesleyan Methodist Church, formed by those who left the Episcopal Methodist Church; the Congregational Church, which arose out of the Presbyterian Church split; May's Unitarian Church of the Messiah; the Baptist Church; and the African Methodist Episcopal Zion (A.M.E. Zion) Church, which was led by Jermain Loguen. Many antislavery lectures were held at the Unitarian Church, and the Congregational Church, established in 1838, became the city's central abolitionist headquarters where most of the large abolitionist meetings would take place.

During the 1840s, antislavery meetings would also convene in the town's city hall, for by then abolitionism had become more acceptable in Syracuse. The organizational activity of the New York Anti-Slavery Society, which by 1836 had spawned 103 local auxiliary societies, and the persuasive words of both local abolitionists and visitors to the city, had made their mark. Fugitive slaves had become a common sight in Syracuse, and they attracted sympathy. Abolitionists became more outspoken and critics of the movement less effusive. Syracuse developed a reputation as a "Hot Bed of Abolition."

• • •

The unique circumstances of the city's development helped to encourage this shift.[9] The town of Syracuse had its beginnings in a small settlement of migrants from New England and New York's Hudson Valley who came to the western New York frontier in the aftermath of the American Revolution. They mined salt from nearby Onondaga Lake, which was endowed along its shores with brine pools created by springs that bubbled up through underground salt beds. In 1794, these settlers established Onondaga County, named, like the nearby lake, after the Native Americans who inhabited the area. As salt manufacturing became more profitable, more settlers arrived, resulting in the creation of the villages of Salina and Syracuse. During the first years of the nineteenth century, Syracuse was the site of several mills, a few taverns, and a general store. A small collection of log homes was sprinkled through these establishments. The village grew

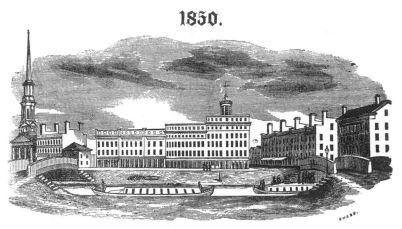

1850.

SYRACUSE, ONONDAGA COUNTY, N. Y.

1850 woodcut of Syracuse, depicting the Erie Canal in the foreground. *From the Collection of the Onondaga Historical Association, 321 Montgomery Street, Syracuse, NY 13202*

exponentially, however, after the 1825 completion of the Erie Canal, which ran through the middle of the town.

The city of Syracuse was a child of the transportation revolution of the early nineteenth century—part of the growth of a national network spawned by the construction of roads, canals and railroads that helped knit the nation together. The Erie Canal gave Syracuse a central position in this new network. By 1850, Syracuse had grown into a full-fledged city due to its location at the confluence of the Erie and Oswego canals, several rivers, turnpikes, and new railroad lines. The log homes in Syracuse gave way to frame houses and some grander federal style homes. A commercial center arose, with gas-lit buildings and horse-drawn streetcars that crowded the dusty roads. Taverns multiplied, and a theater was established. Churches and schools were founded as more and more newcomers arrived. In 1848, Syracuse merged with Salina and was chartered as a city. By 1850, the Syracuse population was around 22,000 people, double that of 1840 and five times that of 1835.

Further aiding its growth was Syracuse's central location between Albany and Buffalo. Syracuse had become known as the central city of New York—a popular destination for holding gatherings and conventions. Political parties, revivalists, and reformers of all stripes held meetings there, politicizing Syracuse residents and exposing them to enthusiastic speakers who advocated change. According to the memoirs of Parish Johnson, who grew up in Syracuse during this period, the town was dubbed the "Convention City," and living there had been a "great school for the youth who desired to keep posted on the affairs of the State and Nation." Abolitionism was one of the topics with which Johnson had early become acquainted, for his hometown was, he said, a noted "abolition hole."[10]

The abolition movement grew. In 1843, a Ladies Anti-Slavery Sewing Society was formed, and its members helped to organize antislavery fairs to raise money for the cause. The New York Anti-Slavery Society held meetings in the city as did the American Anti-Slavery Society. Syracuse also became a primary meeting place for members of the Liberty Party, and many of its state leaders resided in the town. Antislavery conventions were thus a common occurrence in Syracuse. Between 1845 and 1850, the town hosted twelve large antislavery conventions and twenty-five smaller meetings.[11]

The sectional issues that began to intrude on national politics during the late 1840s boosted the antislavery spirit of the town further. As they did throughout the rest of the Northern states, political issues concerning slavery made the citizens of Syracuse increasingly worried about slaveholder influence over the policies of the federal government. Many who did not initially sympathize with the abolitionists' attack on slavery began to adopt antislavery views. In fact, many of the prominent men of Syracuse who had been active in opposing the abolitionists in the 1830s had by 1850 become some of the most vocal antislavery men of the city. Hiram Putnam, E. W. Leavenworth, Vivus W. Smith, and John Wilkinson had all signed a petition opposing the formation of the Onondaga Anti-Slavery Society in 1835. By 1850, they had become outspoken critics of slavery and were at the forefront of the protests against the new Fugitive Slave Law.[12]

As the antislavery spirit grew in Syracuse, some joined the abolitionists. Others became Free Soilers who opposed the expansion of slavery into new areas and who focused their energy on expressing opposition to the Southern slave power and its dominance of American politics. Although not all of the converts to antislavery in Syracuse, or in other areas of the North, were genuine abolitionists who advocated

1851 bird's-eye view of Syracuse.
From the Collection of the Onondaga Historical Association, 321 Montgomery Street, Syracuse, NY 13202

immediate, unconditional emancipation, some abolitionists, including Samuel J. May, saw an opportunity in the antislavery spirit that the sectional politics of this decade had sparked. The North was turning against Southern slave owners, and abolitionists could capitalize upon this sentiment in their drive to eradicate slavery.

• • •

After he arrived in Syracuse in 1845, May played a leading role in organizing antislavery conventions and petition drives in the town. One of the first such meetings had been a protest of the destruction of Cassius Clay's antislavery press in Lexington, Kentucky. This act illustrated one of the big complaints that Northerners made about the institution of slavery in the South: that it was producing a closed society, where freedom of speech and freedom of the press were circumscribed. Antislavery literature was held, undelivered, at the post offices in Southern states, and throughout much of the South it was a crime to distribute this literature or to speak out against slavery. In many states suspected abolitionists were arrested, run out of town, or worse. To question slavery was to expose oneself to bodily harm or even death. Few inhabitants of the South were willing to take this risk.

Cassius Clay was one person who tried to oppose slavery while residing in a slave state, and his experiences illustrate the obstacles faced. Clay was born into a prominent Kentucky slaveholding family. He, in fact, was a cousin to the "Great Compromiser," Henry Clay. As a young man he diverged from his family on the issue of slavery, for he was coaxed into support for emancipation as a young man when he attended Yale College in Connecticut. He supported a gradual end to slavery when he returned home and served in the Kentucky House of Representatives, but his political career was cut short as he lost the support of Kentucky voters due to his antislavery views. He became known in the South as a dangerous radical and as a traitor to his region. He was harassed, and on several occasions he was physically attacked. In 1843, a hired gun shot him in the stomach during a political debate, but he survived, and he was not silenced.

Despite continued threats, in 1845 Clay attempted to establish an antislavery newspaper, entitled the *True American*, in Lexington. Very shortly after commencing operations, a mob of around sixty people broke into his office and removed his printing equipment. Clay was forced to move his paper out of Kentucky to the free state of Ohio.[13]

When news of the Kentucky episode spread into the free states, protests of Clay's treatment emerged, and antislavery activists used the event to publicize the way in which basic constitutional rights were flouted in South. In Syracuse, in September 1845, May and nineteen other Syracuse citizens signed a call for "those who would discountenance the outrages recently committed in Lexington" to meet at the Congregational Church to protest "the unlawful removal of C. M. Clay's press." As with most of Syracuse's antislavery gatherings, the invitation went out to all who sympathized with the cause "without distinction of sect or party." Speakers at the meeting included local Liberty Party leaders like Charles Wheaton and Abner Bates, Garrisonian abolitionists like May, and other men who had been active in the early Underground Railroad like Horace White and William Clarke. Others who took leadership roles at the meeting were not outright abolitionists, favoring instead the promotion of gradual emancipation. One such man was Hiram Putnam, who presided over the meeting. Most of the meeting's officers shared his orientation.[14]

Diverse points of view concerning how activists should attack slavery were therefore represented at the protest meeting, but its participants were unified in their concern about slavery's impact on the constitutional rights of white Americans and on the American Union. They passed meeting resolutions that asserted that "slavery cannot endure the test of free discussion." For that reason slavery advocates were forced to "resort to mob outrage and lynch law, to avert the influence of such discussion." This fact alone showed its "utter incongruity with the essential principles of our free institutions." They complained that the institution of slavery and its influence on Southern attitudes was dividing the nation, "eating out the cement of our union, and sapping the foundation of our social fabric."[15]

Samuel J. May also organized Syracuse meetings to oppose the U.S.–Mexican War. In 1846, as politicians in Washington, DC, met to consider the status of slavery in territories that might be gained from Mexico, May and other antislavery oriented citizens of Syracuse let their representatives know that they did not support the war itself. They believed that no territory should be taken from Mexico and added to the United States.

The protests against the U.S.–Mexican War were not without controversy in Syracuse, however. Although many residents opposed the expansionist war, some argued that opposition to the fight was unpatriotic. The controversy the war provoked among Syracuse citizens came to a climax in June 1846 when the antiwar element issued a call for the "Friends of Peace, of Humanity, and of the Gospel" to meet in protest of the war. Around one hundred Syracuse residents signed the call for the meeting, over which May presided. Once the gathering assembled, however, supporters of the war overtook the meeting and effectively shut it down. Those wishing to protest the war retreated to the Congregational Church, but as they attempted to revive their discussion, a noisy mob gathered outside. At one point, the pro-war faction fired off a canon in order to intimidate those gathered within the church. Through the din of protest and over the threat of canon-fire, the antiwar party continued their meeting and issued peace resolutions calling for the removal of American troops from Mexican territory.[16]

To the satisfaction of the pro-war faction, the government continued to wage the war with Mexico, which ended, in 1848, with the
Treaty of Guadalupe Hidalgo. This treaty brought new territory into
the nation, but it also brought the sectional differences over slavery
front and center in American politics. While Congress debated
Henry Clay's proposal for a sectional settlement, the citizens of Syracuse
continued to hold their own debates about slavery in the territories,
fugitive slave policy, and slavery in Washington, DC.

According to May's biographer, Donald Yacovone, the U.S.–
Mexican War greatly affected the course of May's career as a reformer.[17] As the North and South became polarized over the issue of
slavery, it became clear to May that the rejection of political action, a
position to which he had subscribed as a Garrisonian abolitionist,
was not always practical. As slavery became more and more intertwined with national politics, opportunities to combat the institution arose within the political realm. May thus became more accepting
of political antislavery activism, and this led him to promote a spirit
of cooperation between political and Garrisonian abolitionists in his
state and beyond. Thus, in the years after the war, May became a sort
of bridge between the Liberty Party men and the members of
the AASS.

Although his loyalties remained with Garrison, May felt that cooperation between the AASS and the Liberty Party would aid in
promoting the abolitionist agenda as sectionalism increased in the
United States. Conflict between the political and the Garrisonian
abolitionists had grown during the 1840s as the two groups competed for followers and support. In an effort to promote abolitionist
unity, May encouraged a call for a general state abolition convention
to be held in January 1850 in Syracuse. Garrisonians and Liberty
Party men participated. Garrison was not able to attend, but the
AASS was well-represented, as was the Liberty Party. The *Syracuse
Standard* printed a notice of the meeting on January 8, 1850, informing citizens of the city that a "large amount of talent" would converge
on the city for the gathering. The meeting, the paper announced, was
a way for all abolitionists to come together "during the ensuing session of Congress" to "represent the entire strength of that portion of
our people who are hostile, not only to the extension of Slavery into
new Territories, but to its existence anywhere."[18]

As an expression of unity, however, the meeting was a failure. While May had hoped that abolitionists would join together in one voice on the sectional crisis over slavery, discussions at the meeting degenerated into well-worn arguments between the political abolitionists and the AASS. The main conflict between the two factions, as always, centered on the constitutionality of slavery and the legitimacy of political action as a means of attacking the system. Frederick Douglass said of this debate that it was "one of the strongest barriers against the fusion of the different anti-slavery men into one organization—an end devoutly to be wished for."[19]

Gerrit Smith spoke on behalf of the Liberty Party's position, asserting the antislavery character of the Constitution and the power of politics, while Charles Burleigh argued for the Garrisonians, who believed the Constitution was a pro-slavery instrument. The debate continued for two days and dominated the convention as spokesmen on both sides of the issue weighed in. Essentially, the Garrisonians argued that the Constitution contained immoral compromises that upheld the institution of slavery and gave power to slave owners; slavery thus could not be attacked by political means within the bounds of the country's founding document without legitimizing the immoral contract. Following this argument to its natural conclusion, the Garrisonians were increasingly disunionist, pressing the call for "No Union with Slaveholders." Gerrit Smith responded that the Constitution was subject to the same legal rules of interpretation as all law. The preamble to the Constitution indicated its true intentions, and the document could therefore be interpreted as "not for slavery, but against slavery—not of powers adequate to uphold any part of American Slavery, but powers adequate to overthrow every part of American Slavery." He called the doctrine of no political union with slaveholders "the most glaring absurdity and most superlative humbug imaginable."[20]

The *Syracuse Standard* said of the debate that it was conducted with "masterly ability and adroitness" on both sides, but the paper lamented the way the disagreement dominated the proceedings. "It is understood that the convention was called with the view of reconciling the conflicting opinions entertained respectively by the Antislavery Society and the Liberty Party," it said, "but the result was what everyone predicted, namely no agreement, but if possible, wider separation."[21] May's attempt to unify the abolitionists so that they could work together to move the country toward a broader definition of human rights during the sectional crisis had been frustrated.

· · ·

Questions about slavery and the Union weighed on the rest of the Northern population as well during the first half of 1850. The U.S.–Mexican War broadened the antislavery movement throughout the North as more citizens of the free states came to oppose the expansion of slavery into new territories. The Free Soil Party had emerged in 1848, attracting Northern members of the Democratic and Whig Parties who felt that their party leaders were not taking a strong enough stand against the slave power. The goal of this new party was to halt the expansion of slavery into new territories, and its rhetoric highlighted the way in which slavery interfered with white rights and impeded economic opportunities for white Americans who were not slave owners. While stalwarts like Gerrit Smith held strong to the purity of the Liberty Party's abolitionist goals, some members of his party merged with the Free Soilers, hoping that the battle against slavery's expansion would serve as a starting point for a broader fight that would eventually encompass emancipation throughout the nation's whole. Others, who were either unconcerned with attacking slavery or were convinced that the best hope for change was within the two party system, clung to their Whig or Democratic Party ties. All kept their eyes on the debates waged in Congress over Henry Clay's compromise proposals. Many Northerners, fearing disunion, hoped that the compromise would succeed. Others, however, felt that the new Fugitive Slave Law that was proposed as part of the compromise package infringed too much on the rights of both the individual and the states.

In Syracuse, May and other critics of Clay's compromise proposals held back from organizing in protest against them until May 1850. The compromise resolutions had been submitted to a Committee of Thirteen to iron out the details of the legislation during the spring of 1850, and the Syracuse activists wanted to see what the committee's recommendation would be before outlining their own position. When the Committee of Thirteen sanctioned Clay's plan to combine the territorial question with legislation on fugitive slaves and slavery in Washington, DC, May circulated a call for a town meeting to promote the "unconditional admission of California to the Union." According to the *Syracuse Standard*, the call for a meeting was signed by over six hundred names.[22]

Hiram Putnam called the meeting to order on May 16, and Mayor Alfred H. Hovey chaired the proceedings. May served on the committee that drafted a series of resolutions against the compromise, all of which the meeting approved and published. The resolutions criticized Congress for neglecting regular business due to the "efforts of slaveholders of the South to give priority and predominance to the interests of their local institutions." They stated that it was the "universal and unanimous sentiment of the North" that California should be admitted immediately to the Union with no restrictions. They stated that they had no doubt that Congress had the power to prohibit slavery in the territories, and they strongly opposed the passage of any fugitive slave law that neglected to recognize the rights of the writ of *habeas corpus* and trial by jury given in any free state where a claim was made. They also opposed any guarantee of slavery in Washington, DC, and, due to the hostile climate of the South, called on Congress to protect the security of free state residents who traveled in slave states.

In addition, members of the meeting passed resolutions attacking the process of compromise in general, saying that any compact made by the 31st Congress that would constrain the action of future congresses "can be regarded in no other light than as an audacious assumption of power by one Congress to establish for its successors a rule of action not established by the Constitution itself." Furthermore, they proclaimed that "if the Constitution *was* formed on the plan of compromise of feelings on opinions and principles *then* existing on the question of Slavery, it does not follow that the system of compromise is to be perpetuated to the end of time."[23]

CHAPTER 6

....

Compromise

Although none of them would be present in Syracuse at the time of Jerry's arrest, three national leaders who were involved in the congressional debates over Clay's proposed compromise would become embroiled in the drama surrounding Jerry's case. Two of these men, Millard Fillmore and William Seward, were from towns near Syracuse in upstate New York. The other, Daniel Webster, would make a visit to the region in May 1851 that would contribute to the town's mobilization against Jerry's rendition months later.

While residents of Syracuse formed their opinions on the sectional crisis that followed the U.S.–Mexican War, during the spring and summer of 1850, politicians in Washington, DC—including Webster, Fillmore, and Seward—debated the merits of Clay's compromise proposal. These debates stretched out for months and dominated the proceedings of the 31st Congress. After much conflict, the Washington politicians would eventually agree to what became known as the Compromise of 1850, which included the major provisions of Clay's proposal.[1] The disunion crisis would be averted, but only for a time, and only with a price; for the compromise included the hated Fugitive Slave Law of 1850, a piece of legislation that few Northern leaders would have otherwise supported because of its assault on personal liberties and Northern states' rights.

• • •

Northern politicians were not the only ones who found elements of the compromise unpalatable. Southern ultras also opposed the proposed package of legislation. In the Senate, a Southern opponent of Clay's compromise was one of the first to respond to his proposal. On February 13, 1850, Mississippi senator Jefferson Davis rose to speak in obstinate tones against Clay's plan. His position provides a window into the slaveholder mindset, not only about sectional conflict but about the institution of slavery itself. In his speech, Davis claimed that Clay's compromise was no compromise at all, for it did nothing to alleviate the "sectional domination" of the North over the South. He complained of the Northern "fanaticism" that had "accumulated into a mighty flood," that would eventually pour "turgid waters through the broken Constitution." He then spoke on slavery. He reminded those gathered in the Senate that slavery was an ancient institution that existed in some of the most advanced civilizations in history, and he pointed out that it was sanctioned by the Bible. He went further, arguing that bondage was the natural state for the black man, and that the enslavement of those of African descent in the United States was actually a blessing to the slave because it brought him into contact with Christianity and civilization. This contact, he argued, "would elevate and dignify" his character. Slaves in the United States were improved by their relationships with their masters, who treated them kindly, made them useful, and helped to subvert "the vicious indulgences to which their inferior nature inclines them." According to Davis, freedom for the slaves would mean economic ruin and social instability in the South, where the master would become the slave and the slave would become the master. Davis asserted that the white South could not compromise with the North without risking its own demise, and he demanded a settlement that would protect Southern interests. The North was already "waging war" on Southern institutions by circulating abolitionist literature and aiding fugitive slaves. "Wake before it is too late," he said, "from the dream that the South will tamely submit."[2]

Not all Southerners rejected the compromise. There were congressmen from the South who feared secession, and they wanted a settlement to avert disunion. Henry Foote, who like Davis was from Mississippi, was one of the strongest Southern advocates of compromise, and he sought to promote Unionist sentiment among his colleagues. He called for the special committee to consider Clay's compromise, and he promoted the idea of including all the legislation in one joint bill. Clay worried that the packaging of all the legislation together could lead to its defeat, and he wanted each measure to be considered separately, but, initially at least, Foote's plan won out.

Meanwhile the debate on the compromise continued. Soon it was John C. Calhoun's turn to weigh in on the plan. Everyone was eager to hear what the unyielding pioneer of the Southern rights movement would say. On March 4, when he was scheduled to take the floor, he was too ill to give the speech. Huddled in a blanket on the sidelines, he entrusted that task to his colleague from Virginia, James Mason. As expected, Calhoun's speech echoed the uncompromising tone of Jefferson Davis's. He said that the South had suffered under Northern aggression for long enough, and he declared that California was a test case for the South that would indicate the future intentions of the North. California's admission as a free state would upset the doctrine of political "equilibrium" that had guided the addition of new states since the beginning of the republic. "If you admit her under all the difficulties that oppose her admission," he said "you compel us to infer that you intend to exclude us from the whole of the acquired territories," thus greatly tipping the balance of political power toward the Northern states. The only way the South could then protect her rights, he said, would be to secede from the Union. In order to prevent disunion, Calhoun demanded that the federal government guarantee the slaveholder's right to property in all of the new territories, that it vigorously enforce the Fugitive Slave Law, and that it promote an end to abolitionist agitation. He went further in this speech, calling for an amendment to the Constitution that would "restore to the South, in substance, the power she possessed of protecting herself before the equilibrium between the sections was destroyed by the action of this government."[3]

• • •

During the early part of the debate over Clay's plan, Senator Daniel Webster had remained silent. Webster was a famed orator, one of America's most powerful senators, secretary of state under several presidents, and a gifted lawyer and constitutional scholar. A big man with broad shoulders, dark hair and a piercing gaze, the conservative New Englander had an imposing physical presence that matched his

Daniel Webster.
Photography Collection, Miriam and Ira D. Wallach Division of Art, Prints and
Photographs, The New York Public Library, Astor, Lenox and Tilden Foundations

intellectual might. The American nation waited eagerly for him to address Clay's proposal, but Webster held back. The New England senator, who had built his career on persuasive nationalist speeches and pleas for a strong Union, seemed unconcerned by all of the talk of disunion, viewing it as mere rhetoric. "Things will cool off," he wrote to a colleague, "No bones will be broken."[4]

Henry Clay had paid a private visit to Webster's residence in Washington before he presented his plan to Congress. Although the two Whig leaders were political rivals, both men were known for their commitment to the Union, and Clay wanted Webster's support for the compromise. Clay left Webster's home feeling that he approved of his plan, but for six weeks, as the debate over the compromise raged in Congress, Webster remained noncommittal. His reticence during this early stage of the conflict was no doubt connected to his own political ambition. He had his eyes on the presidency, and at the age of sixty-eight he realized that the upcoming presidential election of 1852 would likely be his last shot at the office. It would not be wise to jump into the fray and stake out a position too early.

Despite Webster's early stoicism, there was a growing sense among many that the nation might be torn apart during these first weeks of debate. Southerners held special conventions throughout the slave states to choose delegates for a larger Southern convention in Nashville, and the threat of secession hung over that meeting. In the North, abolitionists agitated against any compromise with the slave interests, and some of them were advocating Northern secession. A new urgency for compromise in order to quiet the maelstrom grew among Unionists, and, as the controversy lingered, Webster finally became convinced that he needed to weigh in on the state of affairs.

When Webster approached the rostrum on March 7 to address the crisis, the Senate was crowded to overflowing. Webster's eyes were fiery and passionate as he spoke, but he delivered his speech in calm, measured language, articulating each thought carefully. He paused frequently to let his words sink in. He looked at Calhoun throughout the speech, seeming to direct his pleas for unity to the Southern leader. Webster spoke for almost four hours.

Webster's speech was a passionate plea for Union, and it implicitly endorsed Clay's compromise. It was also an unabashed attempt to placate Southern secessionists. Although Webster addressed the grievances that both sections had with one another and called on both to respond to those grievances, he lingered far longer on the Southern point of view, and he seemed to place much of the blame for the current crisis at the feet of Northern abolitionists. It was a lopsided appeal, and it promoted a shocked outrage among Northern antislavery men, who felt that the "Great Dan" had betrayed his principles, for he had always been a critic of American slavery.

Webster's opening to the speech made clear his concern for the Union: "I speak today, not as a Massachusetts man, nor as a Northern man, but as an American." Although he felt slavery was a moral wrong, and he had never supported the expansion of slavery in the United States, he nevertheless believed that uncompromising attitudes about the institution were fueling the division between the North and the South. He asserted that during the time of the Founding Fathers both Northerners and Southerners wanted slavery to end gradually, but the South found it more difficult to extricate itself from this inherited evil from Great Britain. Thus a constitutional arrangement was made to accommodate its continuation. In the aftermath, unfortunately, slavery became "a cherished institution" because of the expansion of cotton, and was no longer considered a "scourge" but instead a "blessing." The extension of slavery had become central to Southern interests.

Now many Northerners were trying "uselessly to reaffirm an ordinance of nature" by demanding that the government exclude slavery in arid territories where slavery was unlikely to prosper. Webster said this demand was seen as a "taunt or reproach" to Southerners who viewed the proposed action as an "indignity" which would take from them "what they regard as a proper equality of privilege." It was provocative to agitate for such legislation. He reminded his audience that his own position had always been one of "no territory," for he knew that the additional lands would force the divisive issue into politics. Now that territory was to be added, both sections would have to find a way to compromise.

He then moved into his discussion of the grievances of the two sections, first of the South and then of the North. Southerners, he said, had some legitimate complaints about Northern antislavery sentiment. First, they complained that the Northern states had not adequately enforced the Fugitive Slave Law of 1793, and on this issue, he boldly proclaimed that the South was right and the North was wrong. The Fugitive Slave Law was constitutional, and thus Northerners had an obligation to obey. Second, Webster said that Southerners complained of antislavery petitions that had gone to Northern legislatures asking them to make declarations against slavery. Slavery in the Southern states had nothing to do with the job of the legislatures of the free states, he said, and he characterized this as yet another needlessly provocative act on the part of Northern citizens. Third, Webster asserted that much of the sectional hostility could be laid at the feet of "abolition societies" of the North. Although they meant well, he argued that "their operations for the last twenty years have produced nothing good or valuable," and they actually worked against emancipation by putting the South on the defensive. After reviewing the sectional grievances of the South, Webster concluded that only one came under the purview of the federal government, and that was the Fugitive Slave Law. This was thus the one area where the North could make a concession to the South in Congress, and he strongly felt that it should do so for the sake of the Union.

Webster also mentioned a few Northern complaints about the South in his speech, but he did not belabor these. He briefly considered the Southern defense of slavery, and the comparisons that Southerners were constantly making between Northern laborers and Southern slaves. He asserted that Northerners rightly found this rhetoric insulting and wrongheaded. The printed version of his speech also referred to the imprisonment of black sailors in Charleston ports. In mentioning these complaints, Webster hoped to preserve a sense of balance, but the speech obviously was meant to appease Calhoun and other Southern secessionists and to ingratiate himself with Southern voters.

Webster ended with a reiteration of the importance of preserving the Union and an assertion that secession could not happen peacefully in the United States. He invoked the Constitution and painted a vivid picture of the chaos that would result if secession took place. "What is to remain American?" he asked, if the Union fell apart.[5]

• • •

Northern critics of Webster looked to Senator William Seward, a "Conscience Whig" with strong antislavery views, to counteract the impact of his speech. Seward was a young man compared to Webster, forty-eight in 1850, and his star was on the rise on the national political scene. Seward hailed from Auburn, New York, a town about twenty miles from Syracuse. He began his career in the New York State Senate, and in 1838 he became the New York governor. In this position, he had supported legislation promoting citizenship rights for African Americans, including the right of suffrage. He also had upheld the state's personal liberty laws, refusing to cooperate with representatives of Southern slave owners who tried to remove accused fugitives from New York to return them to slavery.

William Seward.
*Manuscripts, Archives and Rare Books Division, Schomburg Center for Research in Black
Culture, The New York Public Library, Astor, Lenox and Tilden Foundations*

In the 31st Congress, Seward found himself to be the most outspoken antislavery man in the Senate. Although he was not an abolitionist—he favored a gradual, compensated, voluntary emancipation—Southern slave owners, who had a tendency to associate anyone with antislavery tendencies with the abolition movement, labeled him thus. His speech in response to Clay's proposed compromise would only enhance his antislavery reputation, for the proposed new Fugitive Slave Law had aroused his ire. Auburn, like Syracuse, was an important Underground Railroad depot, and Seward himself had provided refuge for fugitives in his home. The harsh provisions of the proposed revision of the Fugitive Slave Law flew in the face of his position that Northern free states should not be bound to recognize the rights of slave owners within their own state boundaries.

In 1849, Seward took his seat in the Senate, his reputation well established. As he entered the national political scene, he became one of President Zachary Taylor's most influential advisers. In fact, many Washington insiders attributed the Louisiana slave-owning president's opposition to the expansion of slavery in the territories to Seward's influence. In 1850, as the debate over Clay's plan dragged on, many of his fellow senators thus viewed Seward as the president's spokesman in Congress.

Just as Davis and Calhoun proved inflexible in their advocacy for Southern rights, Seward was unbending in his support for the Northern antislavery point of view. When Seward rose to speak on the Senate floor, he pressed that California should be immediately adopted as a free state, lest the nation lose its grip on the territory and with it the ability to promote the spread of free institutions. He argued that the North gained very little from Clay's proposed compromise, for it did not explicitly bar slavery from the territories. In return for the wishy-washy declarations that slavery would probably not flourish in the new territories, the North would be subjected to an unreasonable new fugitive slave policy. In addition it would have to concede to the continuation of slavery in Washington, DC.

Seward was especially critical of the proposed Fugitive Slave Bill, which denied accused fugitives even the most basic legal protections and which encroached upon white Northerners by requiring them to participate in the capture of alleged runaways. He argued that the law infringed upon the rights of Northern states to make their own policies concerning escaped slaves. "The law is to be executed among *us*, not among *you*; not by us, but by the federal authority," he complained. Seward accepted that the bill was within the bounds of the Constitution, which granted the right of recaption of fugitives from labor, but, he said, "There is a higher law than the Constitution." Man's laws should not violate those of God.[6]

Seward's advocacy of "Higher Law" would become the focal point of his speech, and it would be repeated time and again by anti-slavery men who opposed federal fugitive slave policy throughout the 1850s. The terms of the Northern debate on the Fugitive Slave Law had been framed by two men from the same political party, Webster and Seward. It was a battle between "Union" and "Higher Law."

• • •

Clay, Davis, Calhoun, Webster, and Seward had sketched the out-lines of the debate over the compromise. Many others would weigh in on one side or the other over the next few weeks. Finally, members of the Senate appointed the Committee of Thirteen to put together a single piece of legislation. Zachary Taylor jokingly referred to their handiwork as the "Omnibus Bill" because it crammed all the diverse proposals into one vehicle, as Foote had earlier recommended. The name stuck. The Committee of Thirteen met through the last weeks of April 1850, and it produced a report for the Senate in early May. Although amendments were considered in committee, the plan that emerged essentially followed the lines of what Clay had originally proposed.

The obstacle of creating a bill out of Clay's proposal had been surmounted, but now its framers faced debates about whether or not it should be passed. Clay urged it along: "The bill is neither Southern nor Northern," he said, "It is equal; it is fair; it is a compromise." And compromise, he argued, was necessary in order to keep the nation whole.[7] Daniel Webster agreed with him, and he spent much political capital promoting acquiescence to Clay's plan.

Meanwhile, in June, the Southern Convention met in Nashville. The scheduled convention, and the possibility that delegates might promote secession from the Union, had loomed over the compromise debates throughout the spring of 1850, but Clay's proposal had helped to quell the secessionist rhetoric that had been rumbling throughout the South. Although the convention ultimately refused to sanction Clay's plan, the meeting proved to be less dangerous to the Union than many had feared. Some of the Southern "fire-eaters" who were hot for secession still pressed for a rejection of all compro-mise, but most of the delegates hoped that some sort of settlement would provide a solution to the sectional crisis. Thus the radical rhet-oric was toned down at the convention, which promoted a different settlement—the extension of the Missouri Compromise line to the Pacific Ocean.[8]

Despite the calming of the secessionist threat, the convention's lack of support for Clay's proposal was telling. Although the produc-tion of the Omnibus Bill had given hope to Unionists, that hope would soon flounder, for it was destined to fail in the Senate. New political alignments emerged, and forces from both the North and the South that were against Clay's compromise combined as unlikely, temporary allies against the pro-compromise forces. The Omnibus Bill went down in flames, and a weary Henry Clay left Washington to rest, frustrated at the failure of his attempt to work out a sectional settlement.

The failure of the Omnibus, however, was but a temporary setback for pro-compromise forces. Young Stephen Douglas, a Democratic senator from Illinois, revived the life of the legislation by doing what Henry Clay had done with the Missouri Compromise and what he had wished to do with the 1850 package from the beginning— breaking the pieces of the Omnibus Bill into discrete pieces of legislation. To overcome the compromise versus anti-compromise alignment that had taken shape in the Senate, Douglas hoped that he could cobble together alliances between pro-compromise senators and sectional ultras who supported individual pieces of the legislation in order to gain enough votes to push each measure through. This technique proved to be successful.

Douglas's success was helped along by the death of Zachary Taylor in the summer. In early July, the president came down with an acute case of gastroenteritis. On July 9, Washington, DC, mourned his death, but pro-compromise senators also realized that an important barrier to the success of the compromise legislation had been removed. Taylor's veto was no longer a threat.

That Vice President Millard Fillmore would assume the presidency gave even more hope for the compromise's success. Fillmore was a politician from Buffalo, New York, who had been selected as Taylor's running mate in order to bring in Northern votes. As vice president he had found himself alienated and without influence. This sentiment was largely due to his old New York Whig political rival, William Seward, who had gained Taylor's confidence. Fillmore's resentment of his political rival from New York festered while he was in the White House. As president, he was not likely to support Seward's position. Furthermore, Fillmore had long been a political supporter of Henry Clay, and thus it was natural for him to support Clay's compromise. Very soon after assuming the presidency, he rose to these expectations and made it known that this was indeed his position. Reflecting his pro-compromise stance, he appointed Daniel Webster as his new secretary of state when he took office, and Webster helped him to assemble a pro-compromise cabinet. Fillmore and Webster then helped to move the compromise legislation along by using executive patronage powers to build support for passing each of the measures, rewarding those who complied with their wishes.

Zachary Taylor's death was thus an important game changer in the compromise debates. Also important to the outcome was the earlier death of another vigorous opponent to the compromise. On March 31, at the age of 68, John Calhoun succumbed to tuberculosis at Old Brick Capitol Boarding House in Washington, DC. He had pushed his health to its limits in order to weigh in on the sectional dispute, but his body wore out soon after composing the anti-compromise address that Mason had read to the Senate. Jefferson Davis and other Southern congressional acolytes would continue to press the Southern rights argument that Calhoun pioneered, but the "cast iron man" would no longer be a physical force in American politics.

As Douglas had planned, all of the elements of Clay's compromise made it through the Senate as individual measures. California was brought into the Union as a free state. The slave trade, but not slavery itself, was abolished in the District of Columbia. A new, stronger fugitive slave law was passed, and New Mexico and Utah were allowed to organize as territories with no reference to their position on slavery. The legislation was sent to the House, where it passed relatively quickly due to the savvy political wrangling of pro-compromise powerhouses. All of the measures had passed in both houses of Congress by the end of September, and Millard Fillmore signed each piece of legislation into law.

In the Southern states, meetings were called to respond to the compromise measures. Although ultras still opposed giving up any of their Southern rights, the Unionist spirit won out. Most Southerners were not ready for secession, but slave owners still wished to make a stand concerning the legitimacy of slavery. In Georgia, delegates met at a convention and issued a statement that became known as the Georgia Platform, spelling out the state's position on the Compromise of 1850. Georgia, it said, "whilst she does not wholly approve, will abide by it as a permanent adjustment of this sectional controversy," for, the delegates reasoned, the Union had always depended on compromise. It warned, however, that the state "will and ought to resist even (as a last resort) to a disruption of every tie which binds her to the Union," if all of the terms of the compromise were not upheld by the federal government. It made specific mention of the Fugitive Slave Law, saying that the "preservation of our much loved Union" depended upon its "faithful execution."[9] The Georgia Platform became a maxim in the South. Secessionist talk died down, but Southern threats of secession still hovered over American politics. The Union depended on Northerners abiding by all of the terms of the compromise, including the new Fugitive Slave Law.

Many Northerners, fearful for the Union, also wished the compromise to be a "permanent adjustment," but others were angered by its terms and pledged to resist. They were tired of Southern threats. The slave power, which should be weakening in the face of Northern population growth, was using fears of disunion to maintain its grip on the federal government. Northerners were capitulating to unconstitutional and immoral demands for the sake of nationhood.

• • •

By far the most hated piece of the compromise legislation in the North was the new Fugitive Slave Law of 1850. As Butler and Mason had intended when they proposed such legislation, the new law bolstered the Fugitive Slave Law of 1793 by establishing the federal slave-catching bureaucracy that Southerners wanted. New federal commissioners charged with executing the law would be appointed by a U.S. circuit judge, and they would share jurisdiction with federal judges in its administration. These commissioners could themselves deputize marshals to execute warrants, and they also had the power to require Northern bystanders to serve as a *posse comitatus* upon demand. Thus any Northern citizen could be required by law to help aid in the arrest of an accused fugitive. If Northern citizens failed to render aid when called upon, or if they helped a fugitive in any way, they could be fined $1000 or sentenced with up to six months in jail. The law also made all federal officials financially liable for the escape of fugitives from their custody.

Under the new law a slave owner or his agent could themselves detain an accused fugitive, or they could insist that a warrant be issued for the fugitive's arrest by a federal officer. Once taken captive, the accused fugitive was to appear before the commissioner where a summary hearing would take place to consider the slaveholder's claim. The only real questions considered at this hearing were the fugitive's identity and the validity of the slaveholder's claim to his or her person. There would be no jury trial, and the accused would have no right to testify in his or her own behalf. A commissioner would be paid $5 if he released the accused and $10 if he decided on behalf of the slave owner. If the commissioner deemed the slaveholder's claim valid, he would issue a certificate of rendition, and the claimant was protected from any "molestation" by state officials in executing their claim. If a slave catcher believed he could not safely deliver the fugitive to his owner, he could call on the federal government to provide aid at government expense.[10]

The law angered Northerners on multiple fronts. It provided no civil protections at all for the accused fugitives, and it infringed upon white civil liberties by requiring Northern citizens to aid in the slave-catching process. It also quashed state personal liberty laws with a federal law that few Northerners supported and thus bypassed local legislation against slavery. In short, it had made both the government and the Northern populace complicit in the business of slave-catching.

CHAPTER 7

....

Vigilance

Jermain Loguen was especially concerned about the seizure of Jerry under the terms of the new Fugitive Slave Law because of his own status. He was not only a fugitive from slavery himself, he was a very public one who called attention to this fact as he traveled throughout upstate New York giving antislavery lectures. He had gained some notoriety in the region because he had refused the opportunity to purchase his own freedom when presented with the chance, arguing that such an act would give credibility to the institution of slavery. In his antislavery lectures he highlighted his identity as a "defiant fugitive from slavery," and it was well known throughout New York that he had fled from a cruel master in Tennessee. He wrote in his autobiography that after federal politicians passed the Fugitive Slave Law of 1850, he felt he was "more exposed than any fugitive in America to be seized under it," for "not to attempt to re-enslave him was an admission that the government dare not test the strength of the law in such a case."[1] But although he felt vulnerable, the new fugitive slave legislation only compounded his efforts to promote defiance of the federal government's support of slaveholder demands. If the government was to test the strength of the Fugitive Slave Law of 1850, he wished it to fail. Thus, when Loguen heard of Jerry's arrest, he rushed to the commissioner's office in order to lend his aid.

As he approached the room where Jerry was held, Loguen paused to talk with one of the men crowded outside of Sabine's office in the hallway, a fellow black resident of the city. Together they decided that they should attempt to set Jerry free. Although they feared for their own freedom, they concluded that it was time to test the resolve of white men and women in Syracuse who said they opposed the Fugitive Slave Law. "I want to see whether they have courage only to make speeches and resolutions when there is no danger," Loguen's companion said. According to Loguen, "the two men then went up the stairs together, and showed themselves boldly in the presence of the Court, the Marshal, and his armed retainers."[2]

When Loguen entered the room, he saw Gerrit Smith and Leonard Gibbs sitting in chairs beside Jerry. Loguen was familiar with both men through his own connections with the Liberty Party. He and Gerrit Smith were, in fact, close associates who had worked together on a number of projects for black uplift. Loguen arrived just as Jerry was begging Smith to help him escape. Smith was urging patience, promising to help him once support could be mobilized. The crowd outside the courtroom also clamored for Jerry's release, but as yet, there was no plan for how this should be achieved.

Meanwhile Gibbs attempted to delay the hearing by making demands of the commissioner. First, he argued that Jerry should be unshackled and that the armed James Lear should surrender his weapons. Commissioner Sabine responded that he did not have the authority to insist on either action, but he asked that Marshal Allen and Lear voluntarily comply with the requests made. They both refused. Next, Gibbs questioned the validity of the papers identifying Jerry as a slave. Someone other than Lear, he argued, should be present to testify to their authenticity. Sabine overruled this argument. Lear had known both Jerry and his mother personally when he was enslaved in Marion County and therefore was able to corroborate the documents. Out of desperation, Gibbs then insisted that among the papers presented to the officials, there was no documentation proving that slavery was legal in Missouri. No action should be taken against Jerry, he pressed, until this was provided.[3]

While these arguments were taking place, both Sabine's office and the hallway outside became progressively more crowded and confused, and so at 2:30 p.m. the commissioner interrupted the proceedings and called for a half-hour adjournment to look for a bigger room for the hearing. As the crowd clamored outside the office, Jerry raged against slavery and begged for his freedom, saying he would prefer any fate to being taken back to Missouri.

When Sabine announced the adjournment, calls came from the crowd, urging Jerry to make a break for it. Jerry responded. He attempted to escape.

Jerry stood up, lunging for the door, and members of the crowd, "composed mostly of colored persons," grabbed him and pulled him through to the hallway.[4] According to Loguen, "Jerry, with eyes flashing fire, and the strength and agility of a tiger, threw himself across the table, scattering papers and pistols, Marshal and constables, and lay upon the bosom of the multitude."[5] Someone slammed the door to Sabine's office behind Jerry as he exited, and the crowd carried him through the hallway both pulling and pushing him toward the stairs. Jerry, hands bound, fell down the stairs, leading to injuries that slowed his progress. Even so, he made his way out of the building and down Genesee Street and then onto Water Street toward the Lock Street Bridge, which crossed the Erie Canal. All the while he was surrounded by fellow black Syracusans and a few whites who wished to usher him to safety.

When the officials in Sabine's office were able to make their way into the hallway in pursuit of Jerry, the crowd pressed against them, slowing their progress. Prince Jackson, a blacksmith who was one of the town's first black property owners, seized one of the marshals as he left the building, until George A. Green, a citizen whom Marshal Allen had ordered to assist in the recapture of Jerry, forced his release.[6]

Loguen recalled in his autobiography that as Jerry made his way through the streets, "a great multitude, friends and enemies alike, took up the chase in the utmost confusion—the former to assist Jerry and embarrass his pursuers, and the later to retake him." Loguen would later lament that Jerry had acted upon the "hasty advice" that came from the crowd and attempted to make an escape so quickly, with no proper plan for its execution in place. Loguen wanted to enlist the aid of the people of Syracuse who had pledged to resist the execution of the Fugitive Slave Law in their town, for with their assistance, and with a well-thought-out plan, they had much better odds of success.[7]

• • •

If anyone would be able to promote a workable plan to help Jerry, it would be Jermain Loguen. He had arrived in Syracuse in 1841, and

Jermain Loguen.
From the Collection of the Onondaga Historical Association, 321 Montgomery Street, Syracuse, NY 13202

since that time he had been a leader of and spokesman for the town's black community. When he arrived, he found that the members of that community were "comparatively uncared for," and thus he felt it his mission to encourage their spiritual, material, and intellectual uplift. He established a black church in Syracuse, becoming its minister, and he opened up a school where the black youth of Syracuse could learn to read and write. In time, Loguen became an active abolitionist and one of the foremost black members of the Liberty Party, but even as he joined in the biracial effort to end slavery, he always prioritized the local needs of the Syracuse black community. He was determined to promote racial egalitarianism in Syracuse, hoping it would become a place where black men and women could not only live in safety but could flourish. He also became the town's acknowledged Underground Railroad "stationmaster," committing himself to protect and provide for any fugitive that came through Syracuse.[8]

Jermain Loguen had himself fled from the South in 1834, when he was around twenty-one years old. Although he was born into slavery, his mother Jane had been born free in Ohio. Kidnapped by slave catchers as a young woman, she had become the slave of David Logue, who resided in rural Tennessee near Nashville. Sadly, Jane's fate was a common one for African Americans who lived in the Northern communities along the border between freedom and slavery. Slave catchers from the South conducted raids into nearby free territory, alleging their right to do so under the terms of the Fugitive Slave Law of 1793, but they often had no valid claim to persons whom they seized. Black inhabitants of these border regions, whether they were born free or slave, lived in constant fear of being kidnapped. Solomon Northrup, a free black New Yorker who was seized during a trip to Washington, DC, and sold into slavery, helped to publicize the danger that kidnappers posed to free born black men and women with his 1853 memoir, *Twelve Years a Slave*, which was published after his escape from bondage.[9] The vulnerability of free born blacks only increased after the passage of the Fugitive Slave Law of 1850.

When David Logue purchased Jane, he gave her the new name of "Cherry" and treated her as his concubine. He fathered three or four of her children, including Jermain. As a child Jermain, who at the time was known simply as "Jarm," felt that he was relatively well treated on his father's estate, but his situation would change as he entered adolescence. As his mother grew older, David tired of Cherry, and he sold her and her children to his brother Mannasseth to settle a debt. Under Mannasseth, Jarm experienced much abuse. He suffered severe beatings, one leaving his face slightly disfigured, and he witnessed the sale of several siblings, including a sister who had to be chained while she was forcibly separated from her children, all the while begging the slave traders to allow her to keep at least her infant with her. Jarm plotted his escape. When he came of age, he took his master's best horse and, with a companion, undertook the six hundred mile journey to Canada.

He changed his name to Jermain Wesley Loguen in order to provide distance from his slave past, and he set about making a life for himself. After farming in the small settlement of St. Catharines in Canada for a few years, Loguen moved to upstate New York. Eventually, he found work at a prestigious hotel in Rochester, where he was able to save enough money to attend the Oneida Institute, a biracial school run by abolitionist Beriah Green. Once he had acquired the skills that would allow him to raise his own station in life, he set up a school for black children in the town of Utica, hoping to help others do the same.

While Loguen was in Utica, he met Caroline Storum, a free-born black woman visiting from the village of Busti, New York. She had been raised in a household that was active in aiding fugitives from slavery, and, as a fugitive himself, Loguen was interested in doing the same. Their relationship thus became a working partnership dedicated to the education and spiritual uplift of the free black community and to helping fugitives establish self-sufficient, free lives. They married, and a year later the couple settled in Syracuse, where they would raise a large family and aid thousands who came through their town on the Underground Railroad.

Loguen once wrote to his friend Frederick Douglass that under different circumstances he would have been a "very still, quiet man," but instead he found that the events of his life increasingly propelled him to fight against slavery. "Oppression has made me mad," he said; "it has waked up all my intellectual and physical energies."[10] Throughout the 1840s, Loguen, who was an extremely devout man, focused on black uplift not only in Syracuse but also through his itinerant ministry, sponsored first by the American Missionary Association and then later by the African Methodist Episcopal (A.M.E.) Zion Church. In 1844, during his travels through upstate New York, he became acquainted with several white activists for the Liberty Party, including John Thomas, who would soon become the editor of the *Liberty Party Paper* and who would later edit Loguen's autobiography. The Liberty Party men asked Loguen to speak on his experiences as a slave and to stump for James Birney, their candidate for the 1844 presidential election. "In this circuit, his soul became so absorbed with his theme," Loguen said, "as to divorce him, in measure, from the pulpit, and set him beside the slave in a life-long war for liberty."[11]

After the 1844 election, he turned much of his energy to the fight against slavery, and he became known as an effective speaker who was able to stir great emotion as he shared his personal story of enslavement and freedom. Many of those who listened to him commented on the pathos of his delivery, especially as he recounted his reluctance to leave his mother behind in bondage when he made his escape. "What a man you sent me!" wrote Gerrit Smith to John Thomas after he met Loguen for the first time, "I invited him to pray in my family, and he prayed so feelingly for his mother that he set us all in tears."[12]

In 1844 after hearing one of his talks, a group of people in Cortland, New York, decided to purchase Loguen's mother from Mannasseth Logue. They raised funds to send John Thomas to Tennessee to negotiate for her freedom, but the slave owner refused to sell "Cherry" unless Jermain sent additional funds to purchase himself. This provision put an end to the negotiations. Although he did not condemn others who bought themselves out of slavery, Loguen would not resort to the extortion of self-purchase. "I have long since resolved to do nothing and suffer nothing that can, in any way, imply that I am indebted to any power but the Almighty for my manhood and personality," he asserted.[13] Even at the cost of leaving his mother in slavery, Loguen would not break this principle, and the agony of making this decision is reflected in his dedication to aiding others who fled from slavery. In 1848 Jermain and his wife Caroline built their home in Syracuse at 293 East Genesee Street, their permanent address for the rest of their lives, and outfitted it with a special "fugitive chamber" where black sojourners could rest in safety before departing for Canada or to a destination in New York where they would feel reasonably secure. Loguen eventually became known throughout New York as the "King of the Underground Railroad." Caroline was his queen, providing quiet support behind the scenes.

If the failure to rescue his mother encouraged his work with the Underground Railroad, the passage of the Fugitive Slave Law of 1850 transformed this work into a vocation, as greater numbers of anxious fugitives passed through Syracuse on their way to Canada and as he himself became even more vulnerable to re-enslavement. At the time the law was passed, Loguen was in Troy, New York, sent there by the A.M.E. Zion Church to minister to the town's black community. He immediately returned to his home in Syracuse when he heard of its passage in September 1850. Once there, friends and family urged Loguen to either purchase his freedom or to leave for Canada. He refused to do either. Instead, he decided to rally the community of Syracuse, white and black, to defy the law and establish Syracuse as a free space in a slave holding nation.

• • •

Loguen's decision to defy the law was in line with that of many other black citizens of the Northern states. Although the Fugitive Slave Law of 1850 led to a mass exodus of African Americans from the United States for the safety of Canada, many chose to stay put, organizing associations for self-protection throughout the Northern states.

Black vigilance committees, formed in order to give aid to runaway slaves threatened by slave catchers, had existed in some Northern cities since the 1830s. Members of these associations donated supplies to those in need, opened their homes as safe houses, sent warnings throughout the community when slave catchers were about, and even organized groups to confront the slave catchers. At times they sought out white allies to provide legal aid when a fugitive was detained. With the passage of the Fugitive Slave Law of 1850 these societies multiplied throughout the North, and many of them became biracial associations as more and more white citizens showed an inclination to defy the new law.

Unlike their white abolitionist allies, black members of these committees did not have the luxury of debating the merits of government action versus abstaining from politics or the appropriateness of physical resistance to slave law versus absolute nonresistance. Their free lives were at stake, and the U.S. government provided no legal protections or guarantees of safety. Thus, the rhetoric that came from the Northern free black community after 1850 was increasingly subversive, and it often shocked even their closest white allies. Syracuse resident Samuel Ringgold Ward said the new law gave black Americans the "right to Revolution." Black abolitionists who had been closely allied with the nonresistant, antigovernment Garrisonians, changed their views on resistance. "The only way to make the Fugitive Slave Law a dead letter," Frederick Douglass said in 1852, "is to make half a dozen or more dead kidnappers." William Parker, a black vigilance worker in Pennsylvania, summed up the point of view of many free Northern blacks: "The laws for personal protection are not made for us, and we will not obey them." American laws protected white people. "They have a country and may obey the laws," he said, "But we have no country."[14]

A new black vigilance committee had already formed in Syracuse when Loguen returned from Troy on October 3, 1850. Within days of the Fugitive Slave Law's passage, a "Meeting of Colored Citizens" was called at the African Congregational Church, a church recently established by a former member of Loguen's own congregation, John

Lyles. The purpose of the meeting was "to take into consideration the subject of protecting themselves and their families from the slave catcher's and kidnapper's grasp."[15] A crowd of black Syracusans met first on September 20 and again on September 25 in order to organize for self-defense.

At these meetings, representatives of black Syracuse passed resolutions that upheld their right to protect themselves with force, and they repudiated the idea of flight from the United States. They declared that the black population of the city would remain united in support of one another, and they pledged: "We the colored citizens of Syracuse, will join hand in hand and will take the scalp of any government hound that dares follow on our track, as we are resolved to be free, if it is not until after death." American law, they said, had no moral force for African Americans who "have been persecuted by the laws of the land from time immemorial" and "have borne it until forbearance has ceased to be a virtue."[16]

Loguen was absent from these meetings, but he also had taken a public stand against the law. Just before its passage, he participated in an unprecedented "meeting of fugitives from slavery and their friends" in the small Finger Lakes community of Cazenovia, New York, about twenty miles from Syracuse. The Fugitive Slave Convention was held on August 21 and 22, and it was attended by around fifty fugitive slaves and their abolitionist allies. Gerrit Smith had issued the call for the gathering in the name of the New York State Vigilance Committee, over which he presided, and prominent abolitionists from around the state of New York attended. Loguen, Smith, Samuel J. May, Charles Wheaton, and Frederick Douglass were all there.

The presence of so many fugitive slaves in one place was in itself an act of defiance, but the organizers of the convention had arranged to make an even larger statement of protest. William L. Chaplin, a friend of Smith's and an agent of the New York Anti-Slavery Society who had been living in Maryland for several years, was planning to make a grand gesture. He would liberate the slaves of two of the slaveholding congressmen who were pressing for the new law in Washington, DC, and he would bring them in triumph to Cazenovia. Chaplin, however, never arrived. He was arrested in Rockville, Maryland, as he attempted to transport the slaves, owned by Georgia congressmen Robert Toombs and Alexander Stephens, to freedom.

Daguerreotype image taken at the Cazenovia Fugitive Slave Convention, August 1850, by Ezra Greenleaf Weld, brother of noted abolitionist Theodore Weld. Samuel J. May stands behind the man writing at the table. Frederick Douglass leans on the side of the table. Gerrit Smith stands behind Douglass with his arm out.
From the Collection of the Madison County Historical Society, Oneida, NY

Much of the meeting was therefore spent in organizing aid for his defense.

The Fugitive Slave Convention was also notable because of the radical resolutions passed at the proceedings. Frederick Douglass summarized them in his report on the meeting: "The laws of slavery were esteemed but the infernal edicts of pirates—the religion of slaveholders was held to be a horrid and revolting blasphemy against the majesty of Heaven, and a moral war was declared against the law and religion thus specified." In addition, "the ground was distinctly taken in the Convention, that slave laws should be held in perfect contempt; that it is the duty of the slave to escape when he can, and that it is equally the duty of every freeman to help the slave in his flight to freedom when he can."[17]

Loguen chaired a committee of fugitive slaves at the convention, and he and his colleagues issued two addresses—one to the Liberty Party and another to the slaves of the South. Loguen read both aloud, and the second of these, the "Letter to American Slaves from Those Who Have Fled from American Slavery," garnered much attention for its subversive content. Gerrit Smith composed the letter, but it was sanctioned by Loguen's committee as an appropriate expression of their sentiments.

The appeal urged the slaves to try to escape. Although many abolitionists were pacifists who promoted nonviolence in all circumstances, the letter informed the slaves that most of the fugitives from slavery living in the North felt differently. "When the insurrection of the Southern slaves shall take place," it said, "as take place it will, unless speedily prevented by voluntary emancipation, the great mass of the colored men of the North, however much to the grief of any of us, will be found by your side, with deep-seated and long-accumulated revenge in their hearts, and with death-dealing weapons in their hands." The letter instructed slaves that they should not shrink from taking slaveholder property with them to aid in their flight. "For you are prisoners of war in an enemy's country," it said ". . . and therefore, by all the rules of war, you have the fullest liberty to plunder, burn, and kill, as you may have occasion to do to procure your escape." The letter informed them that although many in the North wished to aid the fugitive, there was still danger of arrest and return to slavery once they reached the so-called free states. "But if you make your way to New York or New England," it said, "you will be safe." It predicted that even Daniel Webster would not be willing to chase down a fugitive in these regions where antislavery sentiment abounded.

Although the letter was addressed to the slave, it was just as much directed to white Americans in both the North and the South, putting them on warning about the determination of Northern blacks to protect their own liberty and to aid others who sought freedom. Douglass rightly predicted that the convention's address would "cause a howl to go up from all the bloodhounds of the land," but, he pointed out, the sentiments were the same that any white man would express if he was placed in the same position as the black man.[18]

Loguen returned to Syracuse five weeks after participating in the Cazenovia Convention, and there he found that not only his black neighbors but a large portion of the white residents of town had been aroused by the passage of the Fugitive Slave Law. Soon after the black citizens of the town held their meeting in the African Congregational Church, a call went out in the local newspapers for an interracial, nonpartisan meeting at the town's City Hall to protest the law. Abolitionists conceived of the meeting, but many who participated had not supported the antislavery movement heretofore. The new law had aroused their ire and convinced many that it was time to stand up against the slave power. Illustrating that it was a community-wide protest, the Democratic mayor of the city, Alfred Hovey, presided over the meeting. Newspapers reported that the hall was crowded to overflowing, and the *Liberator* called it "one of the largest meetings ever held in central New York."[19]

Hovey opened the proceedings with a speech. "The colored man must be protected," he said; "He must be made secure among us, come what will of political organizations." He called for residents of the city to "act deliberately" for "this is a righteous and holy cause." Charles Wheaton spoke, informing the meeting, "Your proud state is to be made the hunting ground for the dealers in human flesh." Even worse, he said, "You are, one and all, liable to be called under heavy penalties if you refuse to help retake the fugitives from their cruel oppression." He called the law unconstitutional and called on New Yorkers to rise up against it. Fellow Syracuse abolitionist Charles Sedgewick also spoke, echoing Wheaton's call for resistance and describing the law as the "vilest law that tyranny ever devised."[20]

Participants at meeting expressed determination to resist the government, and they appointed a new biracial vigilance committee of thirteen men, to be led by Wheaton and charged with assuring the safety of the town's black citizens. Those appointed to the committee included city leaders, prominent abolitionists, and leaders of the black community. In her description of this committee, Loguen biographer Carol Hunter points out that it consisted of four lawyers, three newspaper editors, two ministers, and a doctor. Three served on the board of education and eight had held public office. The committee was interracial, nonpartisan, and mostly upper and middle class; it was made up of prominent "molders of public opinion."[21]

Loguen was one of the thirteen. He had arrived in Syracuse just one day before the meeting, and he was an influential voice at the gathering. He gave a rousing speech in which he asked Syracuse residents to defy the Fugitive Slave Law. He shared his own determination to resist re-enslavement at all costs:

> I don't respect this law. I don't fear it. I won't obey it! It outlaws me, and I outlaw it. . . . I will not live a slave, and if force is employed to re-enslave me, I shall make preparations to meet the crisis as becomes a man. . . . If you will stand by me, and I believe you will do it, for your freedom and honor are involved as well as mine, it requires no microscope to see that. I say, if you will stand with us in resistance to this measure, you will be the saviors of your country. . . . Heaven knows that this act of noble daring will break out somewhere, and may God grant that Syracuse be the honored spot, whence it shall send an earthquake voice through the land.[22]

Loguen's request for support was rewarded with strongly worded resolutions against the law. The Syracuse citizens who had gathered in protest asserted that it was the duty of citizens to defy laws that "seriously encroached upon the constitutional or natural rights of the people," and that the Fugitive Slave Law was an example of such legislation. They declared their lack of respect for the politicians who allowed such a law to be enacted, singling out Daniel Webster as especially responsible. "He cannot be called the Defender of the Constitution," they declared, "except in bitter irony." Most importantly, they declared that because the law was "clearly, indisputably unconstitutional," it was "utterly null and void."[23]

· · ·

Jerry's arrest in Syracuse took place one year after this meeting convened, and Loguen hoped that the promises made would be upheld. Members of the town's black community had proved that they were committed to their pledge of self-protection as they led the charge in Jerry's attempted escape from Sabine's office. Lacking in planning and support, however, this initial attempt to liberate Jerry had not been successful.

Jerry's pursuers overtook him at the Lock Street Bridge, and after a violent struggle that left Jerry bruised, bloodied, and with torn clothes, two officers subdued their captive. Jerry's handcuffs remained on, and he begged for their removal as they placed him in leg irons and threw him into a horse cart "like a hog." Jerry cried out repeatedly as he lay in the cart, "Do anything with me, but do not take me back to slavery!" Officers sat astride him to hold him down as they transported him to the police office on Clinton Street, with a large crowd of excited citizens trailing behind.[24]

Syracuse residents that witnessed the manhandling of the fugitive were angered by Jerry's treatment. One witness wrote a letter to his brother describing his feelings about the scuffle: "Soon came a scene that made my blood curdle in my veins; and made me ashamed of the land of my native country; a country of which I had been taught to be proud. I saw this fugitive from, not *justice* but *injustice*, dragged through the streets like a dog, every rag of clothes stripped from his back, hauled upon a cart like a dead carcass and driven away to the police office for a mock trial."[25] According to several narratives, many who had previously encouraged obedience to the Fugitive Slave Law turned against it when they saw the way Jerry was abused. "Jerry's appeals to his captors," one account said, "would have melted any but the hearts of flint."[26] As Jerry was transported to the police office, the church bells in Syracuse resumed their cry that a fugitive needed aid. Now, it was time to test the spirit of resistance in Syracuse.

CHAPTER 8

....

Fugitives

Black abolitionist Samuel Ringgold Ward spent the summer of 1851 away from his Syracuse home, giving speeches throughout the Northern states. He had long spoken up for black rights and for freeing the Southern slave, but after 1850 most of his speeches centered on a more specific topic. "Smarting as we were under the recently passed Fugitive Slave Law," Ward later recalled of this time, ". . . of course this law became the *theme* of most I said and wrote."[1] Agitation against the Fugitive Slave Law had overtaken his life, and by the summer of 1851 Ward had become quite polished in his appeals, for he had been rallying Northern blacks to resist the law and to organize for self-protection for over a year. In October 1851, Ward would return home from his tour. He arrived on the very day that Jerry's arrest provoked a widespread reaction against the law in Syracuse.

• • •

Ward was born a slave in Maryland, but his parents had run away to New Jersey when he was three years old. Fearful of being found by slave catchers, they eventually settled in New York City, where there was a strong black community within which they could find protection. Ward became more familiar with the methods of black self-protection through his association with David Ruggles, the founder of New York City's first vigilance committee. Ward worked in his law office for several years, and he later went on to serve as a Congregational minister and as a teacher in a black school. He became involved with the American Anti-Slavery Society in 1839 but left the organization after the abolitionist schism of 1840 due to his belief in using

Samuel Ringgold Ward.
General Research & Reference Division, Schomburg Center for Research in Black Culture,
The New York Public Library, Astor, Lenox and Tilden Foundations

political means to attack slavery. During the 1840s he became an antislavery speaker and journalist for the Liberty Party, and he settled in Syracuse during the last part of that decade.[2]

Ward was particularly well known for his keen oratorical skills. He was a tall, broad, dark-complected man who commanded the stage, and William Lloyd Garrison said he was among the nation's best antislavery speakers. Early advertisements for Ward's orations referred to him as the "Black Daniel Webster."[3] By 1850, however, Ward had become one of Webster's foremost critics. Ward condemned all political representatives of the Northern states who forced an immoral and unconstitutional law upon their constituents and stripped black men and women of their rights. In April 1850, before the Fugitive Slave Law was passed, Ward gave an impassioned speech in Boston against the proposed legislation. In it he argued that the "infamous bill" was "like all other propositions presented by Southern men," for it "finds just enough Northern dough-faces who are willing to pledge themselves . . . to lick up the spittle of the slavo-crats and swear it delicious." In this speech, he singled out Webster, expressing concern that if Northerners continued to honor him "as a superior mind, and a legal and constitutional oracle," then his "influence upon them and upon following generations will be so deeply corrupting that it never can be wiped out or purged."[4]

After its passage in September 1850, Ward condemned Northern complicity in the institution of the new Fugitive Slave Law, and he used his newspaper, *The Impartial Citizen*, as a platform for encouraging black resistance. He characterized the new legislation as an act of "open warfare upon the rights and liberties of the black men of the North." Because it "strips us of all manner of protection," he wrote, "it throws us back upon the natural and inalienable right of self defense—self protection."[5]

The last place Ward visited in his 1851 speaking spree was Ohio. His wife Emily had accompanied him, and as they wound up their visit to the state in September, they read of an incident involving black self-protection that caused Ward to question his efforts. Perhaps, he thought, he and his fellow black colleagues were fighting a losing battle.[6]

The newspaper reported on a conflict that had erupted near the town of Christiana, Pennsylvania. On September 11, Edward Gorsuch, a planter from Maryland, attempted to recover several of his slaves who had taken refuge at the home of William Parker, a black Underground Railroad operative who resided just outside of Christiana. Gorsuch obtained warrants in Philadelphia to detain the slaves, and then he rode out to Parker's place with a federal marshal and several other men, including his own son. Members of the Philadelphia Vigilance Committee found out about their plans and sent word to Parker about the impending arrival of the slave catchers. When Gorsuch and his party arrived in Christiana, they were thus met with resistance. Dozens of members of the town's black community, along with a few white allies, had assembled to prevent the Gorsuch party from taking the fugitives. Gorsuch did not back down in the face of the crowd, and things turned violent. Gunshots were fired, wounding both Gorsuch and his son—Gorsuch fatally.[7]

It was the response to these events that alarmed Ward. In his view the black participants in this affair were operating in self-defense, but the consequences of their actions were severe. Parker and the men who had taken shelter in his home fled to Canada, but other blacks in Christiana were harassed. The federal government ordered U.S. Marines from the Philadelphia Naval Yard to assist federal marshals in the search and arrest of the men who had confronted the slave catchers. Eventually, they rounded up and imprisoned thirty-eight men. The federal government pushed for severe penalties, and the arrested men eventually faced treason charges, the punishment for which was death.

In his autobiography, Ward states that upon reading the report of the events in Christiana, he handed the newspaper to his wife, "and we concluded that resistance was fruitless, that the country was hopelessly given to the execution of this barbarous enactment, and that it were in vain to hope for the reformation of such a country." After some discussion, he said, "we then jointly determined to wind up our affairs, and go to Canada" where they could enjoy the peace of living in a country without slavery.[8] Ward and his wife left Ohio to return home to Syracuse, where they would begin their preparations to move. They arrived on October 1, 1851, just in time to witness the chaos surrounding Jerry's transport to Police Commissioner House's office following his failed escape attempt.

Ward immediately sprang into action. Perhaps in Syracuse, the law could be defied. Ward went to the building where Jerry was held. There he met up with Samuel J. May, and police officers admitted both men to see Jerry in the hopes they could calm him down. Ward, who could not recall ever seeing a man chained, was taken aback as he saw the shackled fugitive. "Though chained," Ward remembered, "he could not stand still; and in that narrow room, motioning as well as he could with his chained, manacled hands, and pacing up and down as well as his fetters would allow, fevered and almost frenzied with excitement, he implored us who were looking on, in such strains of fervid eloquence as I never heard before from the lips of a man, to break his chains" and set him free.

Ward recalled that Jerry railed against the injustice of his situation. Jerry exclaimed that he was an industrious citizen who had committed no crime, and he lived in a republican nation that was supposed to be committed to justice and liberty. He begged to be saved from a return to slavery, which would be a fate worse than death. He reminded them of the Declaration of Independence and the Golden

Rule and called on them to honor the ideals of both. Jerry's speech moved Ward. Before witnessing the pleas of this man in chains, he said, "I never saw how so hollow a mockery was our talk about liberty and our professions of Christianity. I never felt how really we were all subject to the slave power; I never felt before the depth of degradation there is in being a professed freeman of the Northern States."

Samuel J. May attempted to calm Jerry, promising him that a plan would be made to rescue him. For his part, Ward felt "dumb and powerless." Unable to bear the scene in front of him any longer, he turned to go, but as he exited the building, the crowd assembled outside called for him to give a speech.

Ward felt that his speech could never match the power of the Jerry's words inside the police station, but he stood on the steps in front of the police office building before the angry gathering and made an address. He condemned the execution of a law "pursuant, we pretend, to a clause in the Constitution," to send a man residing in a free state into slavery. "So far are we from 'securing' to him the 'blessings of liberty,' that we have arrested him, confined him, and chained him, on purpose to inflict upon him the curses of slavery." He proclaimed that the term "slave" was an awful one to apply to any American. "How does this sound beneath the pole of liberty and the flag of freedom? What a contradiction to our 'Declaration of Independence'!" Even if Jerry was considered a slave by the federal government, he asked, "Is New York the state to recognize and treat him as such? Is Syracuse the city of the Empire State in which the deeds which make this a day unfortunately memorable, should be perpetrated?"

Ward addressed the crowd for some time, expressing his anger at the oppression of his fellow man and his frustration at his inability to help him. "We hear his strong, thrilling appeals, until our hearts sicken and our heads ache," he said, "but there is none among us that has the legal power to lift a hand in his defense or for his deliverance." He lectured them on the importance of voting for antislavery candidates in future elections: "It is for us to say whether this enactment shall continue to stain our statute books, or be swept away into merited oblivion." At the end of the speech, he met up with his colleague Gerrit Smith, and the two men exited "arm in arm to hold a consultation."[9]

• • •

Ward's plans for flight to Canada would be delayed, for there was work to be done in Syracuse. The outcome of Ward's involvement would restore some of his faith in the willingness of the Northern population to resist the Fugitive Slave Law. It would also, in the end, bolster his desire to flee the United States for the safety of British soil.

Flight to Canada was a common response to the passage of the Fugitive Slave Law. While many black activists encouraged others to stand their ground and fight for their rights, others despaired for their chances of achieving justice in the United States. Church rolls show that many black residents in the free states, including some in Syracuse, ran for Canada as soon as the law was enacted. By 1851, Syracuse had seen its share of fugitives heading in that direction. The journey to Canada was not to be taken lightly, however, for it was dangerous and difficult. Those running from slavery in the South faced almost insurmountable barriers, and because of the terms of the new Fugitive Slave Law, the trek through the free states also held its share of dangers.

Just after the passage of the new law, an incident near Syracuse on the Erie Canal illustrated just how vulnerable the new legislation had made Northern blacks. They were unsafe, even within the free state of New York, and even near the antislavery stronghold of Syracuse.

William and Catherine Harris, a black couple who had been residing in Philadelphia, were among those who decided to leave American soil after Congress passed the tough new law. In late October, with their three-year-old daughter in tow, they boarded a packet boat in Albany, New York, that would take them to Rochester. From there they planned to cross Lake Ontario and make a new home in Canada. They did not complete their trip. Before they could reach Rochester, their daughter would be lost, William would suffer a debilitating injury, and the couple's flight to Canada would be delayed. Their story, as told by Catherine Harris, illuminates the extreme fear that the new law provoked among Northern blacks. Like the Christiana story, it also shows the lengths to which escaped slaves would go in order to avoid being returned to slavery.

The Harris's journey on the Erie Canal did not begin well. When they boarded the boat on which they booked passage, the captain took possession of their tickets and demanded that they pay their fares again. He threatened to turn them in to authorities if they did not. Out of desperation they agreed, but this opening bit of extortion foreshadowed worse trouble ahead.

The captain sent the family to occupy the ship's hold for the duration of the trip. They shared their quarters with buckets of oysters and clams, but they were happy to be on their way. Not long after their journey began, however, two white men—one a crew member and the other an oyster dealer—entered the hold and menaced them. They saw the Harrises, desperate to get to Canada, as easy marks. One of the men told the other that that although they "had not much money now," he expected they would soon "have some money off the niggers," and he winked at the couple. This made them nervous, but they settled in for the night, hoping for the best.

The next morning, the captain came down to talk with them. He told them that "no niggers could pass this canal without being taken," and he and the other white men on the boat repeatedly taunted them with this prediction for the next three days of their journey. The harassment escalated each day, until finally the men insinuated that they had knowledge that slave catchers were waiting to take the Harrises when the boat stopped in Syracuse, laughing at the fear this provoked. Although the men on the boat had fabricated the slave catchers for their own entertainment, and possibly as a way to extort more money from the couple, the Harrises believed their claims.

As the boat moved closer to Syracuse, Catherine Harris turned to her husband and told him that she would not be taken by the slave catchers, whatever the cost. Then, somewhere between the towns of Frankfurt and Utica, she jumped overboard into the water of the canal, her child in her arms. A man from the boat fished Catherine out of the water, but her daughter was never recovered. According to Catherine, the boatmen told her that the toddler had surely drowned, and they did not linger in order to make a search. The boat continued to move westward toward Syracuse.

Grieving for their child and believing that slave catchers waited for them ahead, the Harrises both plunged into despair. William Harris stormed onto the deck of the ship in anger, and the captain threatened to cut his throat if he did not return to the hold. As her husband retreated, Catherine approached the captain and begged him to spare her husband. The captain informed her that he had already sent for authorities, who would come to the boat and "take his head off."

Catherine told her husband about her exchange with the captain, and William said that he would cut his own throat before he would give them the pleasure of doing it. Catherine looked down for a few moments, quiet, trying to decide how to respond. When she looked back up, she saw blood running from her William's neck. He had carried through with his threat and sliced his own throat with a razor. Catherine screamed, but no one came to her aid. William, who feared that he would survive the razor cut, then grabbed a shoe knife and used it to make the cut deeper. As her husband bled, Catherine begged for help. Still, the crew members, playing cards on the deck above, did not respond. The boat continued its journey along the canal.

Finally, just west of Utica, the captain made a stop, but he did not seek aid for Harris. Instead, he put him ashore and left him on land by the canal. William stumbled along the tow path, trying to keep up with the boat. It continued on its way west with Catherine still aboard, begging for someone to help her husband. The boat never stopped. William followed it for some time, blood dripping from his neck, before he fainted on the tow path just outside of Syracuse.

Remarkably, William survived this ordeal. Eventually a passerby saw him lying on the ground, but when he approached him, William roused himself and jumped into the canal, landing under the bow of a canal boat that was passing. He was saved when the captain of the boat, V. R. Ogden of Syracuse, pulled him from the water and brought him into town to seek medical care. Ogden took William to Dr. Hiram Hoyt, a Syracuse physician with abolitionist leanings, and Hoyt dressed his wounds. William had severed his windpipe, but the cuts he had made to his throat were not fatal.

Although William was not able to communicate well as he recovered from his wounds, it was clear that he worried about the fate of his wife. Reverend John Lisle, who was one of the men appointed to the black vigilance committee formed at his African Congregational Church just weeks before, offered to help him find her. He traveled west toward Rochester and eventually located her on a canal boat outside town. He brought her to Syracuse to reunite with William. Once Catherine gave her account of events, officials in Syracuse issued arrest warrants for the captain and the two other men who had harassed her and her husband. Charged with assault and with threatening violence to William Harris, they were detained in Rochester and brought to Syracuse.

At their hearing, the three men gave a different account of the affair, claiming that William Harris had been drunk and disorderly aboard the boat, and that he had convinced Catherine to jump in the water with her child, saying that he would follow them. They claimed that they stopped for an hour to look for the child, and that William had refused to aid in the search. They also testified that William had jumped overboard shortly after slitting his own throat and that he had refused to come back aboard when they attempted to coax him to do so. The jury found their testimony unconvincing, however, and the three men were fined and jailed in Syracuse.

The Harrises eventually were able to continue their journey to Canada, now a family of two instead of three. Their story was widely reprinted in Syracuse and beyond as an illustration of the way Northern blacks could be tormented under the terms of the new Fugitive Slave Law. It captured the attention of Syracuse residents, white and black, and fed the movement to resist the execution of the hated law in their town.[10]

• • •

The Harris story and the Christiana conflict were not the only provocative incidents concerning fugitives that occurred in the months following the passage of the Fugitive Slave Law. Immediately after President Fillmore signed the bill into law, slaveholders like John McReynolds began filing claims with federal officials for the return of escaped slaves. While some fugitives eluded capture, others were caught up in the snare of the slave-catching bureaucracy and removed from their homes in the free states. In most cases the rendition process was carried out smoothly, but there were also episodes of resistance that were widely reported in both the Northern and Southern newspapers. These occurrences made it clear that there was a vigorous opposition to the new law in the North, and they cast doubt on the ability of the Compromise of 1850 to put sectional tensions to rest.

Prominent fugitives who were active in the antislavery movement were especially vulnerable, for they could be easily located. An episode in Boston that occurred just as the law was passed illustrated the danger that activist fugitives like Jermain Loguen and Samuel Ringgold Ward faced. William and Ellen Craft, a couple who had escaped from slavery in Georgia two years earlier, had also felt threatened by the provisions of the new Fugitive Slave Law. Their escape, which involved light-skinned Ellen disguising herself as William's master and traveling with him by steamship to free territory, was well known. The Crafts frequently addressed antislavery audiences, regaling them with the story of their daring flight from Georgia. Because of their activism, their former owner knew they were living in Boston, but he was not sufficiently motivated to try and recapture the couple until after the new Fugitive Slave Law provided support for the rendition process. The difficulties of successfully reclaiming fugitives in New England had been too daunting before September 1850.

The Craft's former master moved quickly, however, once Congress passed the new law, sending agents to Boston in order to bring them back to him. Word spread once these agents came to town, and the abolitionists went to work. Antislavery men began organizing a legal defense for the fugitives, and the Boston Vigilance Committee posted handbills throughout the city warning of the slave catchers who had come to town. As a result, the men who came for the Crafts experienced constant harassment as they searched for their prey. They eventually left Boston, having failed in their mission. After this episode, the Crafts fled to Canada and from there traveled to Great Britain in order to avoid further attempts to return them to Georgia. They spent many years promoting abolitionist sentiment on the other side of the Atlantic, returning to the country only after the end of the Civil War.[11]

Meanwhile in New York City, James Hamlet became the first Northern black person successfully detained under the Fugitive Slave Act of 1850. When news spread of his arrest on September 26, black neighbors of the thirty-one-year-old porter held a meeting at Mother Zion Church in New York in order to raise the money necessary to purchase Hamlet's freedom from his claimant. Antislavery whites showed up to offer their support as well. This biracial effort was a success, and after nine days in jail, Hamlet returned to his home, his freedom purchased.[12]

Many fugitives were not as lucky as Hamlet or the Crafts. According to Stanley Campbell's classic study of the enforcement of the Fugitive Slave Law, most fugitive claims made by slave owners in federal courts led to the return of the fugitive to their owners at government expense.[13] Even so, public episodes of resistance continued to occur, especially in the antislavery stronghold of Boston. In February 1851, the first widely publicized rescue of a fugitive slave from custody took place in that city. Shadrach Minkins was a Boston waiter who had fled from slavery in Norfolk, Virginia. On February 15, two officers seized him and took him to a nearby courtroom for a hearing to determine his status. When they heard of the arrest, antislavery-oriented attorneys mobilized in order to legally challenge Minkins' detention. They had little hope of success, however, under the terms of the new law. While this "antislavery bar" was attempting to use legal tools to free Minkins, black members of the Boston Vigilance Committee took matters into their own hands. Hundreds of black and white protesters had gathered outside the courtroom where Minkins was held. Before a hearing to determine Minkins's status could be completed, between twenty and thirty black men pushed out of the crowd, stormed the room, overpowered Minkins' guards, and liberated the fugitive from custody. Members of the black community hid Minkins in their Beacon Hill neighborhood, and from there he traveled along the Underground Railroad network to Montreal, where he lived out the rest of his life, a free man.[14]

The rescue of Shadrach Minkins was a challenge to the federal government—a message that black Americans would not submit meekly to a law that violated their rights or to a government that offered them no protection. As celebrations of the rescue took place throughout Boston, it was also evident that many white Northerners would support resistance to the law. Federal officials rushed to respond to the event, hoping that they could prevent it from becoming a precedent for further trouble.

Daniel Webster was particularly embarrassed by the Minkins rescue, which took place in his hometown, and he doubled his already vigorous efforts to encourage Northerners to support the new Fugitive Slave Law. Henry Clay called for a congressional investigation of the rescue. Southerners, as well as Northerners that wanted the Compromise of 1850 to be respected, urged Millard Fillmore to order federal troops to aid in the execution of the law. Fillmore would follow this advice in future cases. He also called for the vigorous prosecution of the men who had rescued the former slave from custody, and federal officials complied, issuing indictments for those who took the lead in removing Minkins from the courthouse. The government ultimately would be unsuccessful in punishing the rescuers. Because the Boston jury was unsympathetic to the government's case, none of defendants were found guilty.

With the rescue of Shadrach Minkins, many Bostonians hoped that they had proved that the Fugitive Slave Law could not be executed in their city. They were proved wrong, however, a month and a half later. On April 4, 1851, a seventeen-year-old runaway slave from Georgia named Thomas Sims was detained in Boston. Again a crowd assembled outside the courtroom where the fugitive was held, and talk of a forcible rescue circulated among black Bostonians. This time, however, authorities were determined that no rescue would take place. The courtroom was tightly locked down, and federal troops were dispatched to aid local officials and ensure that order prevailed. White abolitionists tried to secure Sims' freedom with legal arguments, but they were unsuccessful. After it was determined at the federal hearing that Sims should be returned to Georgia, rows of several hundred U.S. Marines marched the black teenager to a warship waiting in the U.S. naval yard. The federal government transported Sims south, and upon his return, his owner immediately sold the rebellious slave. Sims ended up in Mississippi, where he would remain enslaved until he was able to gain his freedom in 1863, after which he fought for the Union army during the Civil War.[15]

• • •

In the Sims case, and later after the Christiana conflict, the federal government had made the point that it was serious about enforcement of the new law. Its actions, however, only heightened the indignation of Northerners who hated it. The dispatch of the military was seen as a tyrannical act employed in order to enforce a tyrannical law, and anger about the overreach of the federal government increased. Comparisons to the British troops that occupied Boston during the Revolutionary Era abounded. When treason charges, punishable by death, were brought against the Christiana prisoners in 1851, anger was further heightened. Northern black activists, and growing numbers of whites, called louder than ever for a revolution against an unjust government that was under the sway of the slave power and that was failing to protect the natural rights of all of its citizens.

When Jerry was arrested in Syracuse in October 1851, conflict over his fate would be added to the list of events that inflamed the nation during the months after the Fugitive Slave Law was passed. If Boston could not be the place from which no fugitive could be taken, the antislavery residents of Syracuse thought, perhaps their city could.

CHAPTER 9

....

Protest

After the recapture of Jerry, Commissioner Sabine scheduled the resumption of his hearing for 5:30 p.m., but crowds of people remained outside of the building that housed the police office. Members of the Syracuse Vigilance Committee met in the early afternoon to discuss Jerry's predicament. They decided to reconvene later in the day at the office of Dr. Hiram Hoyt on South Warren Street. It could accommodate both the committee and any additional people who wished to render aid. Gerrit Smith, Samuel J. May, Jermain Loguen, and Samuel Ringgold Ward were among the two dozen men who were present at Hoyt's office when this meeting began "at early candle light." The main subject of discussion was whether to rely on legal proceedings to free Jerry or to try to affect a forcible rescue.

Gerrit Smith believed that Jerry was likely to be set free. Commissioner Sabine's reluctance to enforce the law was well known; and just a month before Alfred Conkling, judge for the Northern District of New York, ruled a rendition effort in Buffalo invalid, asserting that the Fugitive Slave Law should be applied only to slaves who ran away after the passage of the law. The same argument could apply to Jerry. Smith did not consider a legal judgment an ideal outcome, however. "The moral effect of such an acquittal will be nothing to a bold and forcible rescue," he argued. He pressed that a successful rescue would "demonstrate the strength of public opinion" against slavery and the Fugitive Slave Law. It would "honor Syracuse and be a powerful example everywhere."[1]

Both Jermain Loguen and Samuel Ringgold Ward had made known their support for the use of force in defense of the rights of black men and women, and so Smith's suggestion sat well with them. May, a Garrisonian peace man who had always promoted nonresistance, hesitated; but in the end, he went along with the decision to enact a rescue. "If any one is to be injured in this fray," he said, "I hope it may be one of our own party."[2]

May's caution governed their final plan, which combined resistance with nonviolent tactics. They would have a horse and buggy stand ready near the police station. At a prearranged signal, they would break into the police office building, press on those guarding Jerry without using violence, remove him from the building, and take him to the waiting buggy. They would instruct all those involved to avoid injuring anyone. After Jerry was taken, they would drive him randomly through town and then return to a prearranged spot to conduct him to a hiding place in Syracuse, since all the town's exits were likely to be guarded. Once this plan was made, hardware merchant Ira Cobb and the Reverend L. D. Mansfield, both vigilance committee members, were sent to the courtroom to monitor events so they could give a signal to begin. They planned to act sometime around eight o'clock.

Meanwhile, at the police office, the officials holding Jerry discussed how to maintain order. Anxious about the crowd gathered around the building, Marshal Allen demanded that Onondaga County Sheriff William Gardner call out the militia. Gardner explained to the marshal that as sheriff he could not legally call out the military unless there was a riot, but he would ask them to stand ready at their armories. At around 4:00 p.m., Gardner called on the National Guard, the Syracuse Citizens Corps, and the Washington Artillery to stand by.

When news of these orders reached Vigilance Committee member Charles Wheaton, he went to the National Guard Armory and argued that the sheriff had no authority to assemble the troops. He assured them that if they marched on the citizens of Syracuse, they would be prosecuted for any violence committed, and he told them they should immediately disband. There was some resistance to Wheaton's demands at the armory, but Colonel Origen Vandenburgh, head of the 51st regiment of the National Guard, came to his aid, clarifying the sheriff's lack of authority. The troops were sent away. Soon afterward, the Syracuse Citizens Corps also disbanded. The only force that remained available was the Washington Artillery under Captain George Saul, who was decidedly unsympathetic to the Fugitive Slave Law.[3]

Two great factions were making their plans, both with a determination to define the character of Syracuse. Antislavery forces hoped to uphold the city's reputation as an abolitionist stronghold and a place where no fugitive could be sent back to slavery. Those opposing them wanted to uphold the town's reputation for law and order. A showdown was soon to take place between these two groups, which had been clashing with one another in Syracuse ever since the Fugitive Slave Law had been enacted.

• • •

On May 26, 1851, Secretary of State Daniel Webster had visited Syracuse as part of a larger tour of upstate New York. Webster, along with President Millard Fillmore and other members of his cabinet, ostensibly made the trip through the state in order to celebrate the completion of the Erie Railroad, but in reality the tour was an opportunity to promote obedience to the Fugitive Slave Law among residents of the Burned-Over District. For Webster, the tour was also an opportunity to gather support for his upcoming presidential bid. He hoped to promote an image of himself as the savior of the Union, a portrait that had always served him well politically.

After visits to a number of New York towns with the president's entourage, Webster made the second half of the tour alone. He had separated from the presidential party in Buffalo due to an illness contracted by his son Fletcher, who had accompanied him on the trip as his personal aid. After attending to Fletcher, the secretary of state followed in the president's wake, five days behind him, giving speeches in Buffalo, Rochester, Canandaigua, Auburn, and then Syracuse.

A group of Syracuse "Friends of the Union" were especially eager to hear Webster speak. When Fillmore had arrived in their city on May 21 with Attorney General John J. Crittenden and Secretary of the Navy William A. Graham, they had given a dinner in honor of the visitors. Fillmore, hoarse and weary as his tour of New York wound down, gave no big address during his visit. Comments on the sectional controversy were limited to a short speech by Graham, who urged the people of Syracuse to "cast aside all local fanatical feelings," or else face the danger of civil war.[4] Hoping for a more extensive statement from the government, these Friends of the Union wrote to Webster and encouraged him to give a powerful speech on the necessity of compromise when he came through Syracuse.

Thirteen-year-old Parish Johnson attended Webster's Syracuse speech on May 26, and decades later he recorded his memories of the famed orator's appearance as he addressed a large Syracuse audience from a the small balcony of Frazee Hall. Webster overlooked a green space in Market Square where thousands gathered to hear him. "I remember as he spoke he steadied himself by holding on with both hands to the iron railing of the balcony," Johnson said, "that his large body was clad in a blue swallow-tailed coat with brass buttons; that a vast head with a dark, impressive face, deep cavernous eyes, which occasionally flashed like the embers of a smoldering fire, was presented to the people." He also described the Syracuse audience, which, he said "gazed with awe and listened with bated breath" while Webster explained why he had made the infamous speech of March 7, 1850, that called on Northerners to compromise with Southern slaveholders. "In his deepest tones and most measured accents," Johnson said, Webster built to a crescendo, until he forcefully insisted to those gathered before him that the law would be enforced throughout the North. Those who resisted the law, he angrily exclaimed, were guilty of treason. Attempts to nullify it were in vain, even in the antislavery stronghold of Syracuse. Johnson remembered that "a long murmur of dissent went up from the assembled thousands" when Webster made this claim.[5]

• • •

After his speech, some in his audience speculated that Webster had overindulged in drink at his lunch earlier in the day and that this was the reason that his Syracuse address was particularly antagonistic.[6] Whether or not this is true, Webster had a reason for singling out Syracuse in his speech, for agitation against the Fugitive Slave Law had remained vigorous in the city in the months after the initial October 4 indignation meeting was held to protest its passage. Antifugitive slave law meetings continued to convene in the city into the spring of 1851, and criticism of the law remained strong in the city's press.

One of the law's most vigorous critics in Syracuse was the *Syracuse Standard*, a Democratic newspaper with a decidedly Free Soil slant (it supported the antislavery "Barnburner" wing of the Democratic Party, but it would shift its support to the Republican Party in 1856). Much of its commentary focused on the questionable constitutionality of placing enforcement of fugitive slave policy in the hands of the federal government, and the paper strongly advocated the Northern states' rights to determine slave policy at home. Editorials in the paper argued that the Constitution granted no "express authority" to Congress to legislate on fugitive slaves. "Slavery is a State institution, so the South has always insisted," one writer pointed out, "and in this view of the subject, the North has acquiesced." Thus, "it is not for Congress to make laws respecting it; that work belongs exclusively to the states." The passage of the Fugitive Slave Law violated this proposition by declaring "slavery to be a national instead of a local institution, subject to the control of Congress, and not the States in which it unfortunately exists."[7] In other words, slave owners could not have it both ways. If Congress had the power to dictate fugitive slave policy in the North, it also had power over slave law in the South and thus the ability to abolish slavery. If slavery was truly a local institution, then Congress had no power over policies concerning slavery in any of the states, and that included the rendition of fugitive slaves in the Northern states that had abolished slavery.

Although criticism of the Fugitive Slave Law was widespread in Syracuse, not all residents opposed it. The Friends of the Union were insistent that the law must be obeyed. Most of those who urged their fellow citizens to support the legislation followed the same lines of reasoning as Daniel Webster. As their name implied, they feared for the fate of the Union if the Compromise of 1850 failed. The *Syracuse Star*, a conservative Whig newspaper, became the mouthpiece of Webster's supporters in Syracuse. It responded to the rebellious rhetoric in the *Standard*, calling for support for the new law even among those who disagreed with its fairness. Writers for the *Star* argued that both the fate of the nation and the reputation of Syracuse were at stake.[8]

In November 1850, one month after the initial Syracuse protest of the Fugitive Slave Law had taken place, the Friends of the Union called a meeting of "Patriots" at City Hall to counteract the agitation that brewed against the law. At the meeting, they issued resolutions approving all of the "measures lately passed by Congress, particularly the Fugitive Slave Bill," and they praised Henry Clay, Daniel Webster, and Millard Fillmore for making the Compromise of 1850 possible. Unwilling to let this meeting take place uncontested, anti–Fugitive Slave Law people showed up and protested the resolutions that endorsed the Compromise of 1850. Sitting in the back seats of City Hall, these men, numbering between fifty and a hundred, loudly exclaimed "No" when a vote was called on the resolutions. The chair of the meeting, Moses D. Burnet, simply ignored them and announced that the resolutions were adopted by "a large majority."[9]

Jermain Loguen, in his autobiography, called the Friends of the Union meeting a failure.[10] An editorial in the *Syracuse Standard* ridiculed the proceedings, saying it was a "humbug" to assert that the Union was endangered by opposition to the law. "No respectable party, either in the North or the South, is opposed to Union," it said. The Southern fire eaters and the Northern Garrisonians "have no sympathizers among the masses and never will have." Thus, "fighting disunion is fighting a shadow—a chimera." It argued that "it is time lost, worse than wasted, for sensible men to get together and make speeches and pass resolutions on this subject."[11]

• • •

The rhetoric against the Fugitive Slave Law, however, quickly took on a more revolutionary tone in Syracuse. In part, this was due to Syracuse's role as a convention town. In early 1851, abolitionists in the city hosted several large meetings to protest the legislation, feeding the opposition to the law. In January, the New York State Anti-Fugitive Slave Law Convention was organized by Syracuse abolitionists. Another gathering to protest the law met in March, and in May the American Anti-Slavery Society held its seventeenth annual anniversary meeting in Syracuse. Opposition to the Fugitive Slave Law of 1850 was the dominant theme at each meeting, and at them one can see the way in which abolitionists seized the issue of the Fugitive Slave Law of 1850 in order to advance their cause.

New York Liberty Party men dominated the first meeting, and Garrisonians from New England were the primary movers at the other two, but factions from both groups were present at all the events. The usual disagreements between the two groups, therefore, arose as members from each side debated how the recent fugitive slave legislation shed light on the appropriateness of political action among abolitionists, the constitutionality of slavery, and the sanctity of the Union. Despite these disagreements, at these meetings both Garrisonians and Liberty Party men acknowledged the fundamental unity of their goals. They all hated slavery and believed it should be abolished unconditionally, and they all believed that the Fugitive Slave Law lacked legitimacy and should not be obeyed.

The New York State Anti-Fugitive Slave Convention, which met January 7–9, was the first state convention in the nation to be held in opposition to the law. "The passage of this bill has made it plain," the call for the meeting stated, "that liberty and slavery cannot subsist together; and has forced upon our country this great question: Shall tyrants thenceforth rule this Republic, or Freemen?" That Daniel Webster promoted such an act, it said, "confounds us with astonishment." The call for the meeting was signed by the leading Syracuse antislavery men, including Samuel J. May, Charles Sedgwick, Charles Wheaton, Ira Cobb, and John Thomas. In their call, these men expressed the desire to provide a model for meetings in other Northern states. They wanted to send Congress the message "that *they have waked up the lion*" and "that they must recede from the daring encroachments that they have made upon Northern sentiments and Northern liberties—must annul that wicked Bill—or consent that it must be at once a *dead letter,* or expect to see this American union deluged in blood."[12]

In addition to those who called the gathering, other important New York abolitionists—including Frederick Douglass, Gerrit Smith, Jermain Loguen, and William Chaplin—were all present at the January convention. Each of the men gave a rousing speech on the need to resist the Fugitive Slave Law.

Gerrit Smith answered the "Patriot" crowd who insisted that the law must be obeyed, whether or not one agreed with it, out of respect for the Constitution and the American government. "Constitutions and laws, so far as they are repugnant to truth, are void," he said. Because slavery "abrogates all things which go to distinguish law, it is no law." Following in line with the Liberty Party platform, he argued that the Constitution was never meant to give the government the power to "reduce any human being to bondage." He asserted that "when civil government violates the law of God, it is utterly without authority." Therefore, he said, "it is not rebellion—it is not treason to resist such a law" as the Fugitive Slave Law when it "commands that which we cannot obey, without disobedience to God."

The presence of William Chaplin, recently released from his Baltimore jail cell, was particularly celebrated at the meeting. Jermain Loguen gave a speech on behalf of all the fugitives from slavery welcoming him and expressing gratitude for his service to those fleeing from bondage. Chaplin thanked Loguen, and he spoke to the convention about the need for all antislavery men to go beyond rhetoric in their opposition to the Fugitive Slave Law and to be willing to back up their words with action. "If you say the Fugitive ought not go back, then do not suffer him to go back," he said.

Also celebrated at the convention was the presence of the nation's most famous fugitive from slavery, Rochester's Frederick Douglass. Douglass served as president of the convention, and his speech shocked many, for the former Garrisonian minced no words as he called for violent resistance to the new law. He addressed the convention, "The question before us is *whether we are to make resistance to the execution of this law?*" His answer: forceful resistance to the Fugitive Slave Law was necessary, and "the Convention should say so." Douglass said that he advocated the use of moral suasion when it was sufficient to accomplish change, "but if any one should attempt to take me into Slavery, I should strike him down—not with malignity, but as complacently as I would a bloodhound, and think I was doing God a service." He pointed out that "the South knows how to keep abolitionists away—they say they will hang them on the next tree." Likewise, "this Convention ought to say to slaveholders that they are in danger of bodily harm if they come here and attempt to carry men off into bondage." He urged active resistance to the law; for in order to show the federal government and the slave power that the kidnapping of black men and women from the North would not be tolerated, they must set an example. "If in Syracuse you allow one to be taken off," he said, "another will soon follow."[13]

On March 5 and 6, there was another meeting, a "Great Anti-Slavery Convention" to welcome British abolitionist George Thompson, who had just arrived to the United States to give antislavery lectures. Thompson was affiliated with the AASS, and much of the meeting had a Garrisonian tone, but Gerrit Smith presided over the proceedings and welcomed Thompson to Syracuse.

Twenty resolutions were passed at this meeting, justifying resistance to the Fugitive Slave Law. Among them was a condemnation of the hold that slaveholders had over federal policy. They projected that as long as slaveholding was recognized and upheld as a constitutional right, the South would "by an inevitable necessity, shape the legislation and dictate the policy of national affairs." Another declared that Daniel Webster, in promoting the new law, was a "paid traitor of freedom."

Thompson gave a rousing speech at the meeting, and at its end Samuel J. May took the stage with four black men and one black woman, all recent fugitives from slavery. "Citizens of Syracuse," he asked, "will you defend with your lives, if need be, these defenseless and hunted children of God?" There was a resounding "Aye!" from the audience. May then asked for volunteers to provide aid and employment for those standing on the stage, and although such provision was illegal under the new Fugitive Slave Law, arrangements for each of the fugitives were procured within fifteen minutes. Those who provided aid allowed their names to be publicly announced.[14]

Protests against the Fugitive Slave Law of 1850 continued in Syracuse at the convention to celebrate the seventeenth anniversary of the American Anti-Slavery Society on May 7–9. The AASS broke from the tradition of holding the anniversary meeting in New York City when it gathered in Syracuse. The annual convention usually was held at New York's Broadway Tabernacle, but in 1851 they were denied access to the building. William Lloyd Garrison blamed the influence of the city's "Union Committee," which had been pressing for obedience to the Fugitive Slave Law, as well as the widespread fear of "mobocratic" action that might surround their meeting.[15]

The abolitionists of central New York, headed up by Samuel J. May and Gerrit Smith, responded to this situation with an invitation to the AASS to hold their gathering in the City Hall of Syracuse. Residents from throughout the town would provide accommodations for the out-of-town abolitionists who would be attending the meeting. Although many in Syracuse, including Smith and the other Liberty Party men, disagreed with the Garrisonians on the question of political action and the constitutionality of slavery, they neverthe-less once again welcomed them to central New York.

There was some debate at the meeting on the different views of the two abolitionist factions, but all in all, those present agreed that the Fugitive Slave Law, if not the Constitution of the United States, lacked legitimacy. "As for the Fugitive Slave Law," one resolution of the meeting proclaimed, "we spit upon it; we trample it under our feet." Another asserted that "we will oppose the slave hunter when-ever and wherever he makes his appearance among us, and give succor to the flying fugitive in defiance of all Presidential proclamations and government penalties."[16]

• • •

Thus, when Webster visited Syracuse, just a little over two weeks after the AASS anniversary meeting, he had a point to prove. Although, as Samuel J. May indicated in his autobiography, much of Webster's two hour speech was simply a "rehash of his infamous speech in Congress on the 7th of March, 1850," the secretary of state also sought to com-municate that he and other members of the Fillmore administration considered resistance to the Fugitive Slave Law, such as had been pro-moted at the meetings in Syracuse in the months before, to be trea-son.[17] "I tell you if men get together and declare a law of Congress shall not be executed in any case, and assemble in numbers to prevent the execution of such law," he said, "they are guilty of treason and bring upon themselves the penalties of the law." He then addressed the abo-litionists' meetings against the Fugitive Slave Law that had taken place in Syracuse and made a forecast: "They say the law will not be exe-cuted. Let them take care, for those are pretty bold assertions. The law must be executed, not only in carrying back the slave, but against those guilty of treasonable practices in resisting its execution. Depend upon it, the law will be executed in its spirit and to its letter. It will be exe-cuted in all the great cities; here in Syracuse; in the midst of the next Anti-Slavery Convention, if the occasion shall arise."[18]

Webster's prediction would soon be put to the test. The next major antislavery convention in Syracuse would be the state Lib-erty Party convention that met on October 1, 1851—on the day of Jerry's arrest.

CHAPTER 10

....

Rescue

After federal officials recaptured Jerry in such a brutal manner, the news captivated the people of Syracuse. Throughout town, groups of people loitered in the streets, talking with one another about Jerry's arrest, his failed attempt at escape, and what might become of him. Rumors flew about the city, that the proceedings against him had been part of a government conspiracy to fulfill Webster's prophecy of the previous spring. Had there been some sort of plan to make sure that the Fugitive Slave Law was executed in Syracuse, as Webster had predicted, "during the next antislavery convention"? Was Jerry's arrest on the day of the New York State Liberty Party Convention planned, or was it a poetic coincidence? Whatever the case, one half of Webster's prophecy had been fulfilled. The real question on everyone's lips was whether the second half of it would be as well. Would the law be fully executed? Would Jerry be returned to slavery?

In a report to Frederick Douglass on the events surrounding the Syracuse Liberty Party meeting that met on the day of Jerry's arrest, John Thomas echoed the mood of the town. He wrote that "the threat of Daniel Webster in his mad speech made here last summer" had "fallen back with things memory laid aside" when the abolitionists met. "It was almost forgotten," he said, but it was quickly recalled by everyone at the meeting when Charles Wheaton had come through the door of the Congregational Church with the news that a fugitive slave had been taken in the city. Thomas speculated that it had been the "intention of the government to disturb the ordinary business of our convention." It had succeeded, and thus "so far Mr. Webster gained his point." But, Thomas asserted, the actual enforcement of the Fugitive Slave Law was "quite another thing."[1]

Thomas had until recently been editor of the Syracuse-based *Liberty Party Paper*, an organ funded by Gerrit Smith to promote the party's ideals in the face of the forces of compromise that had swept the North. Thomas had moved from the town of Cortland, New York, to Syracuse in order to run this paper, but he had little success in attracting enough subscribers to keep afloat. Consequently, in the summer of 1851, Thomas and Smith made an agreement with Frederick Douglass to merge Douglass's Rochester-based antislavery newspaper, the *North Star*, with the *Liberty Party Paper*. The new paper, co-edited in its first year by both Thomas and Douglass, was called *Frederick Douglass' Paper*.[2] The merger was a great boon for Smith, Thomas, and the Liberty Party. Douglass's name lent prestige to the publication, which made for a larger readership for Liberty Party writings. The merger also would cement the new alliance between Douglass and the political abolitionists that gradually had been forged after the black abolitionist had split away from Garrison and the AASS.

From Syracuse, Thomas reported the events of October 1, 1851, for *Frederick Douglass' Paper*. Gerrit Smith had presented a number of resolutions from the Business Committee to the small gathering, and they were all unanimously adopted. Among them had been proclamations that a civil government should protect human rights and that a true one "instead of enacting laws for slavery, tramples upon them, and instead of patronizing slaveholders, punishes them." Another resolution stated that "the fugitive slave law is no law, and conveys no authority to them who act under it." Those who enforced it were "naked kidnappers." Yet another referred to the recent shooting of Gorsuch in Pennsylvania, comparing the Christiana affair to Lexington and Concord: "If it were wrong of the men of Pennsylvania to shoot, in order to save themselves from slavery, it was infinitely more wrong in the men of the Revolution to shoot, in order to save themselves from taxation."[3]

The meeting had just passed these resolutions when Charles Wheaton interrupted the proceedings to tell them of Jerry's arrest. Excitement abounded. Here was an opportunity for the abolitionists to back up their words with action. Syracuse could provide the setting for yet another revolutionary act.

Thomas told Douglass of the energetic procession to the office of Commissioner Sabine after Wheaton informed the Liberty Party convention of the arrest. When Thomas himself arrived to the room where Jerry was held, the sight of the bound fugitive surrounded by armed men, he said, "nearly blinded my eyes and deranged my senses." He looked upon the scene of Jerry's first hearing for a short time, and then, "tired with my position and the disgusting exhibition," he went to City Hall, a quarter mile away.

Shortly after he arrived at his destination, he heard a "tempestuous roar of human voices passing by." Among the voices he heard several crying, "Stop the kidnapper!" Soon the voices died off, and someone remarked that Jerry was safe. Just as he breathed a sigh of relief, however, Thomas heard voices approaching from the east. He saw Jerry returning, "the upper part of his abused body dressed only with irons, being lugged along in a manner most insulting to decency and humanity, while hundreds of indignant citizens were circling around him and his insolent captors." He recalled that Police Commissioner Sylvester House consented "very reluctantly" to Jerry's placement in his office for the resumption of his hearing. Once there, officials readied themselves for the new proceedings, and a crowd gathered outside of the police office building, which was situated on Clinton Square in the heart of the city, overlooking the Erie Canal.[4]

At 5:30 p.m. Commissioner Sabine resumed Jerry's hearing in Police Commissioner House's office. Two new men had arrived to assist in Jerry's defense, Hervey Sheldon and D. D. Hillis, of Syracuse. Earlier in the day, Hillis had addressed the crowd outside the police office, assuring those present that legal arguments would be used to free Jerry. Now he took the lead in the attempt to make good on this promise. As James Lear presented his case for Jerry's rendition, Hillis interrupted him frequently with questions about Jerry's status. He then repeated Gibbs's earlier demand that Lear bring documentation proving the legality of slavery in Missouri. He argued that slavery could not exist in common law. Echoing the famous *Somerset* case, he asserted that "the presumption in favor of freedom must be overcome by some positive law of Missouri authorizing the relation of master and slave in that state."[5]

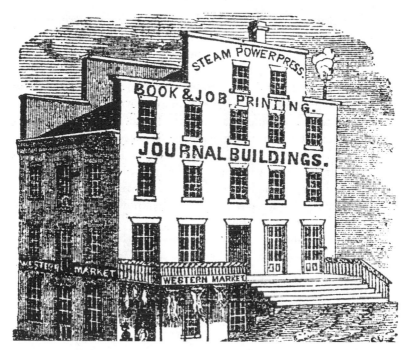

Raynor Block Building, that housed the police office where Jerry was taken after his first escape attempt. It would later become known in Syracuse as the Jerry Rescue Building. It was demolished in 1974.
From the Collection of the Onondaga Historical Association, 321 Montgomery Street, Syracuse, NY 13202

After Hillis presented this argument, the hearing did not progress much further, for with the resumption of the proceedings, the crowd outside, numbering between four and five thousand people, had grown more restless. Inside the building they could hear loud shouts for Jerry's release, and it became difficult to talk over the noise. Soon stones and other objects crashed through the windows of the police commissioner's office. The officials inside debated whether they should continue their proceedings. Marshal Allen, hoping to expedite the process of rendition, insisted that they persevere, but when a large stone narrowly missed Sabine's head, the federal commissioner called another recess until 8:00 a.m. the next morning.

The federal marshals took Jerry into a small room in the back of the police office, turning on the gas lights so that they could keep an eye on the prisoner. James Lear and several other men accompanied them. Most were there to help guard Jerry, but also present were Ira Cobb and Reverend Mansfield. They had been allowed to attend Jerry's hearing after they left the vigilance meeting at Hoyt's office, and they had remained in the building afterward. Cobb was able to station himself by the gas light in the room where Jerry was held.

Commissioner Sabine, Marshal Allen, and the lawyers defending Jerry left the building to make their preparations for the next day. Allen later recalled that he had to don a disguise in order to make his way through the crowd gathered outside safely. He also said that he had assumed Jerry would be transported to a nearby penitentiary. He would not have left the police office had he known that Jerry would remain inside the besieged building.[6]

After Jerry's hearing was interrupted for the second time, the crowd outside dissipated, but a healthy assembly of people remained. In his letter to Douglass, Thomas estimated that there were between two thousand and three thousand people in front of the building as nightfall approached, and other witnesses corroborate this guess. Alert black faces dotted the mostly white crowd, for Jermain Loguen had urged members of the town's small black community to be present and ready for action. Thomas noted that many bonnets and parasols were scattered around the assembly, marking the presence of women as well as men.[7]

At 8:00 p.m. members of the Syracuse Vigilance Committee, as planned, joined the throng of people in front of the police office. They mingled with the crowd. Soon after their arrival, someone shouted, "Now!"

At the signal, a group of men rushed out of the cluster of onlookers and attacked the building. They were armed with clubs, axes, and iron bars that Charles Wheaton had not so discreetly placed outside his hardware store earlier in the evening. According to one news report, "the chief movers of the crowd appeared to be negroes," but both black and white men participated in this assault on the police office.[8] Some observers noted that a number of the white men had blackened their faces and hands with burnt cork. Whether this was done as an expression of solidarity or as an attempt to disguise their appearance is unknown. Most likely, it was a combination of the two motives.

The rescuers smashed the windows, chopped and pried out the casings, and removed bricks from the building in order to gain entry.

Inside, in the room where Jerry was held, Ira Cobb extinguished the gas lights. So far all was going according to plan. The Vigilance Committee had made its move, and they were abetted by the crowd. The drama of the attack on the building increased when several men who had not been part of the planning committee in Hoyt's office arrived with a ten-foot-long wooden beam. One of the men carrying this object, William L. Salmon of Oswego, New York, yelled "Old Oswego is coming!" as they beat down the door of the building with their makeshift battering ram.

The door collapsed, and Jerry's rescuers pressed into the building. Instead of going directly for the door of the room where Jerry was held, the rescuers aimed the beam at the partition between Police Commissioner House's office and the back room where Jerry was held. As they began to batter at the wall, Henry Fitch, a federal marshal from Rochester, exited through the door of the room where he had been guarding Jerry and fired two warning shots. When he did this, someone hit his gun arm with a rod of iron, knocking it from his hand. Fitch rethought his plan to face down the crowd, turned to the nearest window and jumped from the second floor of the building onto the canal path below. He emerged with a broken arm, either from the blow or the fall. The other men who had been guarding Jerry pushed their captive out of the back room, slamming the door behind him and assuming postures of self-defense.

Two black men, Peter Hollinbeck and William Gray, grabbed the prisoner. Jerry was still shackled at both his wrists and ankles, and so they carried him out of the building and down the street. As they exited, crowds of people swarmed around them.

The crowd followed the men carrying Jerry through the city, away from the police office, past the Syracuse House hotel and onto Watson Street, stopping near Hiram Hoyt's medical office where James Davis, Jason S. Hoyt, and Moses Summers waited with a one-horse buggy that would take Jerry away. One of the city's aldermen, B. L. Higgens, attempted to block the procession, demanding that the crowd disperse and Jerry be handed over. Moses Summers, who was the editor of the *Syracuse Standard*, knocked Higgins out of the way and told him not to interfere with the escape. At first, because it was surrounded by so many people, the buggy holding Jerry could not move. The rescuers shouted "Fire! Fire! Fire!" in order to disperse the crowd. From a nearby corner, the Washington Artillery fired its canon and a round of warning shots, which aided the rescuers. The crowd cleared, and the carriage was able to take Jerry away, embarking upon a circuitous path to the predominantly black, eastern part of the city.

The plan hatched at Hiram Hoyt's office had been carried out, helped along by concerned black and white citizens who had been gathered around the police station. When he reported the events of the rescue to Frederick Douglass, John Thomas said that there appeared to have been no organization or advance planning involved. He thought the crowd had acted spontaneously. But the Jerry Rescue was no haphazard affair. Had it been the result of spontaneous mob action, the scene would have been more chaotic and, it is likely, more violent. The rescue of Jerry was an intentional act of civil disobedience and not, as critics later would claim, the act of a mob. For his part, Thomas, who "stood at a convenient distance, but in full moonlight view of the whole transaction" wrote to Douglass, saying that he believed the rescue was "the sublimest scene my eyes ever beheld."9

• • •

Lucy Watson was sixteen years old at the time, but in later years she clearly recalled Jerry's arrival at her home on the night of October 1. Lucy had been born free, but her grandmother was born a slave, and Lucy took an interest in the fate of runaways who came through the city. She had been ironing when, earlier in the day, she heard the church bells signaling that a fugitive had been taken. Like most of the other members of her community, she ran into town when she heard the alarm and stayed there as the events surrounding Jerry's rescue unfolded. As she returned to her home in the basement of the house on Irving Street that evening, she was surprised to see a carriage standing in front of the house. Jerry was there with some of his rescuers. She knew one of them, a black man named William Thompson, whose nickname was "Dare Devil." Thompson told her that Jerry needed aid, and so she and her sister helped to carry the frightened man into their home. Jerry was bruised and his face was bleeding. He explained his injuries to her, saying that he had taken a large stone in the forehead when the frightened officers had shoved him out the door of the back room of the police office building and into the approaching crowd.

Lucy tended to Jerry's wounds, washing them with whiskey. He was still shackled, and so the next order of business was getting his leg irons off. They had some difficulty, but finally they were able to remove them with a hammer and flat iron. Lucy helped to bury them in the back garden. She was anxious, she said, "for we knew it was high treason if we were discovered." Next they went to work on the handcuffs, but they were more difficult. They were forced to enlist the aid of a nearby blacksmith, Peter Lilly, who was an abolitionist. Lucy recalled that he "was so excited when he found that we had Jerry that he could scarcely file them." After removing the handcuffs, Lucy helped to dress Jerry in a disguise of women's clothing and then, she said, they "boosted him over the back fence, and that was the last we saw of him."[10]

After leaving Lucy Watson's place, Jerry spent time in several other residences of the black community; but Jason Hoyt and James Davis, who had taken charge of his care after the rescue, worried that Jerry would be easily discovered if he remained in any of these homes. They decided to move him to a less obvious hiding place: the residence of Caleb Davis, who lived just off of Genesee Street on Orange Street, very near the police station from which Jerry had been liberated. Davis was the town butcher, and he was known throughout Syracuse as a vocal anti-abolitionist Democrat who "never met the sweet-tempered Samuel May in public without reviling him." Davis, however, had been angered by the calling of the militia, feeling it was an abuse of power and an attack on the personal liberties of the people of Syracuse. He also had been sickened when he witnessed the sight of Jerry being dragged to the police office after his first escape attempt. He agreed to help Jerry, and the fugitive stayed at his home for four days to recuperate from his injuries. During Jerry's stay the surly butcher frequently appeared in Syracuse "on the street cursing the abolitionists and the whole business."[11]

After Jerry had time to recover from the events of October 1, Jason Hoyt and James Davis made arrangements to move him out of Syracuse. Most officials in town assumed that Jerry was already beyond their reach in Canada, and so things had calmed down in the city. News of his escape, however, had been telegraphed to villages

throughout upstate New York. Federal marshals in the region remained vigilant, and Hoyt and Davis remained cautious. When they
retrieved Jerry from Caleb Davis's home, Hoyt came armed with a
gun, and he gave Jerry an iron bar. If anyone should attempt to interfere, Hoyt said to Jerry, "you will strike to kill; I will shoot to kill."[12]

In his autobiography, Samuel J. May describes the scene of Jerry's
final escape from the town. Jason Hoyt and James Davis "were seen to
help a somewhat infirm old man into the vehicle, jump in themselves
and start off at a rapid rate." Suspicions were aroused as they quickly
drove out of town, and they were pursued for eight or ten miles. They
were able to lose their pursuers, however, because James Davis had
bribed a toll-gate keeper on the Cicero plank road, which ran north
out of Syracuse. The toll-keeper opened the gate for Jerry's buggy, but
when those following behind him arrived, he "appeared to be sunk in
his final slumber, so slow was he to respond to their call."[13]

Jerry was deposited at an Underground Railroad station about
thirty miles away in Mexico, New York. From there he was sent
sixteen miles west to Oswego, where he stayed until it was safe to board
a ship that would cross Lake Ontario, bound for Canada. Jerry made it
safely across the border, settling in the Canadian town of Kingston,
where he worked as a cooper and carpenter, as he had in Syracuse.

• • •

During the time in which Jerry lay low in town, the Liberty Party
rejoiced at the action that had been taken. At 9:00 a.m. on the day
after the rescue, party members reconvened the meeting that had
been interrupted by the exciting events of October 1, its attendance
greatly increased over that of the previous day. At it, Gerrit Smith
made a speech on the notion of "Law." He told the convention that
the men and women who had aided in the liberation of Jerry would be
branded as criminals, but that those who labeled them as such had no
conception of what true law was. True law "came from the bosom of
God," and supported "the harmony of the universe." Enactments like
the Fugitive Slave Law "came from hell to derange the harmony of the
universe," and thus "could not be law."[14] In his communication with
Frederick Douglass, John Thomas wrote that several new resolutions
had been added to those passed the morning before, praising the

actions of those who had proved Webster's prophecy wrong by aiding in the rescue of Jerry. All were unanimously adopted. Gerrit Smith presented them to the audience, and among them was the following: "Resolved, that we rejoice that the city of Syracuse—the antislavery city of Syracuse—the city of antislavery conventions—our beloved and glorious city of Syracuse—still remains undisgraced by the fulfillment of the satanic prediction of the satanic Daniel Webster."[15]

CHAPTER 11

Reaction

On Sunday, October 19, 1851, thirty-five-year-old Syracuse house-wife and mother Ellen Birdseye Wheaton wrote in her diary of the impact of the Jerry Rescue on her town. "For the last fort-night," she penned, "our little city has been the scene of great excitement and agitation, resulting from an attempt to carry into effect the Odious Fugitive Slave Law." Little else had been discussed in the days since the rescue, and she noted that many rumors were afloat. No word had yet come out "as to the course of the Government officials," but there was much speculation about who would be indicted and about whether or not they would face treason charges. Ellen paid close attention to the rumors, for her husband Charles was a member of the Syracuse Vigilance Com-mittee and, she said, "Charles confidently expected to be arrested."[1]

She hoped that he was wrong. Although Charles Wheaton played a key role in the events of October 1, he had not participated in the libera-tion of Jerry from the police office building. At the time of Jerry's escape, he had been at fellow abolitionist Charles Sedgwick's law office prepar-ing paperwork for a kidnapping complaint he intended to file against James Lear. This alibi, however, did not alleviate Ellen's worry. "The pro-ceedings of the U.S. District attorney are as secret as possible," she wrote, "and everything wears the appearance of injustice and knavery."[2]

• • •

Ellen and Charles Wheaton had moved to Syracuse from the neigh-boring town of Pompey, New York in 1835. They were both reform-minded people who were involved in the temperance and abolition movements. Charles had been one of the founders of Syracuse's abolitionist Congregational Church, and he was a popular antislavery singer who graced many abolitionist meetings with his music. He was a member of the Liberty Party, and he had been nominated as the party's candidate for several minor state offices over the years. He also owned a hardware store in town just off the Erie Canal, which he had established in partnership with his brother Horace, a Free Soil–oriented Democrat who had recently become the mayor of Syracuse.

Between his reform work and his business, Charles was often away from home, leaving Ellen to care for their household and their children, ten of whom had been born by October 1851. In her diary, Ellen recorded her feelings of loneliness and isolation during Charles's frequent absences, but she also expressed pride in her husband's altruism. And although she was often absorbed with her household duties, Ellen also was involved in many reform activities herself— attending meetings, lyceums, and conventions for various causes.

Both Charles and Ellen were committed reformers, but Ellen experienced a growing sense of anxiety after Congress passed "the Odious Fugitive Slave Law." On February 24, 1851, after hearing the news of the Shadrach Minkins rescue in Boston, she wrote that the events in "that goodly city" had "cast a gloomy shadow" over her thoughts. Especially troubling, she said, were "the president's proclamation calling on all good citizens to help execute this infernal law, & a second message sending a large body of the military, to aid in enforcing the law." She wondered about Syracuse: "How long will it be ere we shall be partakers in such scenes?" And she worried about her own response: "When equal excitements, & risks will be met with here, Have I courage and firmness equal to the crisis? I tremble in fear, at the prospect." She was especially anxious, however, about Charles's reaction to such an event, for he had been at the forefront of the Liberty Party's agitation against the Fugitive Slave Law in central New York. "I fear for my husband whose ardent and fearless temper I so well know," she wrote, and she predicted that "he will be in the midst of danger when it comes."[3]

Her prediction was correct. Although Charles Wheaton had not been among the crowd of men that stormed the police office, he played a strong supporting role in Jerry's rescue. He had warned the Liberty Party men that a fugitive had been taken. He had participated in the vigilance meeting at Hiram Hoyt's office. He had stacked supplies outside his hardware store to be used in the rescue. He had convinced the militia not to assemble during the hours before the rescue. And in the aftermath of Jerry's liberation, he would continue to encourage resistance to the Fugitive Slave Law in Syracuse, even as there was talk of prosecuting the rescuers for treason, a crime that was punishable by death.

Although Ellen worried about the possibility of her husband's arrest, Charles hoped for it. He believed that no New York jury would issue a guilty verdict for violation of the Fugitive Slave Law, much less for treason. A trial would only help the abolitionist cause by gathering more attention to the Northern opposition to slavery and the hated law. Other abolitionists who had been in Syracuse on October 1 felt the same way. In the week after the rescue, Samuel J. May, Gerrit Smith, and Charles Wheaton all took public responsibility for their roles in planning the event.

Other participants in the rescue, however, were more worried about their fates. Black rescuers found themselves in a particularly vulnerable position. Not only were they subject to prosecution for roles they had assumed in defying the Fugitive Slave Law, but for them there was an additional danger: the publicity from the rescue might attract the attention of slave catchers, who would then come for them and try to take them south. After the rescue there was a thus a small exodus to Canada. Some of the exiles, like Vigilance Committee member J. M. Clapp, were white; but most of them were black men and women who feared the slave catcher as much or more than they feared prosecution for defying the Fugitive Slave Law.

Jermain Loguen, who had always resisted suggestions that he should remove himself to the safety of Canadian soil, finally capitulated. Just after the rescue, he left his family in Syracuse and took refuge in St. Catharines, Ontario, where he stayed well into 1852. Other black Syracusans also fled to Canada. Rescuers William Johnson and Peter Hallenbeck also went to St. Catharines, and according to the records of the Syracuse Wesleyan Methodist Church, several black couples resigned their membership on October 20, 1851. Beside their names in the membership rolls was the notation: "Removed to Canada to escape slave catchers!!"[4]

Samuel Ringgold Ward, who had considered leaving for Canada with his family before the rescue, acted upon his earlier plans in its aftermath. In a letter to fellow Canadian fugitive Henry Bibb, he wrote "I am, like yourself, a refugee." He explained that he had run because he feared arrest for treason, and he told Bibb that he planned to make Toronto his home. "In the spring," he said, "I may be a candidate for a job of hoeing in your garden."[5] In his autobiography, Ward gives further explanation of his decision to leave the United States: "I could not remain in that country without repeating my connection with and participating in such an affair as I was then guilty of."[6] Ellen Wheaton mentioned the flight of the Ward family in her diary, saying that she was "both sorry and ashamed" about their situation.[7]

Some fled the city in the aftermath of the rescue, but many stayed and waited to see how the government would respond. Federal officials immediately took depositions after the events of October 1, but no arrests were finalized for two weeks. Joseph Sabine took the lead in the interviews—his last act before resigning his position as federal commissioner. James R. Lawrence, the district attorney for western New York who had represented the government at Jerry's rendition hearing, was asked to evaluate the interviews and determine who should be arrested. Lawrence faced a difficult task. He had received a letter from U.S. Attorney General John J. Crittenden with instructions from President Fillmore insisting that "the supremacy of the laws must be maintained at every hazard and sacrifice."[8] Now Lawrence had to decide who was to be held responsible for an act perpetrated by a crowd that "had no head nor end."[9] On October 9, in a report on the lack of immediate government action following the rescue, the *National Antislavery Standard* speculated that the government was stymied because "the treason this time is that of a whole city."[10]

As Lawrence deliberated, rumors circulated. Crittenden's letter to the district attorney was printed in New York papers, and the people of Syracuse speculated about who would be arrested and under what charges. Most believed that Gerrit Smith, Samuel J. May, and Charles Wheaton would be among those who were indicted. In the end, however, the district attorney did not target the prominent abolitionists who planned the rescue. Instead, Lawrence ordered the arrests of men pinpointed by witnesses as having participated in the actual removal of Jerry from custody.

The first round of arrests took place in mid-October. Those arrested were listed and described by the *New York Tribune*: "Ira H. Cobb, merchant; Moses Summers, of the *Onondaga Standard*; James Davis, a Nephew of Gov. Davis of Mass.; Stephen Porter, butcher; William L. Salmon (Granby, Oswego Co.) farmer; Harrison Allen (colored) hired man; William Salmon (colored) school teacher; Prince Jackson (colored) farrier."[11] They were all ordered to appear at a preliminary hearing before federal Judge Alfred Conkling in Auburn on October 15, where he would determine the charges they would face. Ellen Wheaton wrote in her diary of the arrests. She noted that she was encouraged by fellow abolitionist William Crandall to attend the hearing at Auburn. "I cannot go," she wrote, "I wish I could."[12]

Crandall was upset about the planned hearing in Auburn. Before the arrests had taken place, he had written an open letter to Lawrence urging him to bring those arrested before Commissioner Sabine in Syracuse to determine the charges. The cost of traveling to Auburn, he argued, was unnecessary. In addition, he pressed to have Sabine hold a hearing "to its fullest extent" rather than convening a grand jury to make indictments. A grand jury would "just mean lining the pockets" of government officials and increasing the cost of defense for the indicted by several hundred dollars. "Do you wish, so far as in you lies to establish in Syracuse a 'reign of terror' such as the most infernal despotisms in the world have ever sought?" he asked. He likened the removal of the accused from Syracuse for indictment proceedings to the holding of a "secret tribunal, where perjury can run riot."[13] Crandall's pleas fell on deaf ears. The government was not about to leave the fate of the rescuers in Sabine's hands. When the first arrests took place, Crandall posted a flier around the city, informing all of Syracuse that the railroad had agreed to half-price fares to Auburn for the term of the hearings, and he urged as many people as possible to go to the city to show their support for the defendants.

After the arrests, others in town expressed their contempt for the government's decision to prosecute the rescuers. According to newspaper reports, after Millard Fillmore's letter to D.A. Lawrence was made public, one set of Jerry's shackles were placed in a "neat mahogany box" and sent to the president, "care of the Onondaga County Fair."[14] In Auburn, a group of Syracuse women who attended the hearings of the accused gathered up thirty three-cent bits— "thirty pieces of silver"—which they sent to Lawrence. The package was labeled "the price of innocent blood."[15]

In addition to the question of who would be arrested and where they would be indicted, the issue of what charges the government would file was a great topic of discussion in Syracuse and beyond. In his speech in Syracuse the previous May, Webster had warned the audience that he considered defiance of the Fugitive Slave Law to be treasonous. After the Christiana affair in Pennsylvania, his statement was backed up by the government when it charged thirty-seven persons associated with the resistance with that crime. Now everyone wondered if the government planned to follow suit in Syracuse. The *National Era*, a newspaper based in the nation's capital, predicted that it would. Once this trend gained momentum, it said, "hundreds of other cases will follow." There was a great sense of alarm expressed at this possibility. "Does the Government really suppose that it can hang all these hundreds of indicted citizens," it asked, "without provoking civil war?"[16] In a letter printed in *Frederick Douglass' Paper*, John Thomas commented on "the attempt to cover with the bloody code of treason all forcible attempts to secure freedom for ourselves and others." He said that "the penalties of the Fugitive Slave Law are bad enough, without adding to them the infamous death penalties of the law of Treason."[17]

The *Syracuse Standard*, however, expressed less concern about the threat of treason indictments. On October 11, it reported a rumor that President Fillmore was pushing federal authorities to make this charge. It dismissed such talk, however, as "mere political bravado and chicanery." It quoted Article III, Section 3 of the Constitution: "Treason against the United States shall consist ONLY in levying war against them, or in adhering to their enemies, giving them aid and comfort." Trying those who defied a federal law for treason rather than for violation of the law in question was clearly unconstitutional, it argued.[18]

As the government men deliberated on the arrests, and as the nation gossiped about the possibility of treason charges, the Syracuse abolitionists organized a "County Rally for Freedom," held at the

Syracuse City Hall on October 14 and attended by around five hundred people. At the meeting, Samuel J. May gave a rousing speech and attendees formed a finance committee in order to raise money to help with the defense of those arrested in conjunction with the rescue. The meeting then passed resolutions that congratulated the people of Syracuse for the Jerry Rescue, declared that it had been an honorable act, and expressed their lack of respect for government officials who had become slave catchers. Each of these resolutions ended with the declaration, "If this be treason, let it be treason."[19]

On October 15, the day after the county convention, Syracuse citizens learned of the first arrests and the hearing in Auburn. The abolitionists responded with another gathering that morning at the Congregational Church. Charles Wheaton opened the proceedings, announcing the need for the community "to be making common cause in response to the arrests." The meeting, like the rescue, was biracial. It was led by white abolitionist Enoch Marks and black lawyer, abolitionist and poet, George B. Vashon, and it was attended by a "large and respectable" audience. Two resolutions were passed at the gathering. One pledged to show "that we are law abiding citizens, by bearing patiently any evils that our government may implicate upon us." Another pledged monetary and moral support for those who were indicted by the government for participation in the Jerry Rescue. Before adjournment, they formed a new organization in the city, a "Jerry Rescue Committee," with the specific purpose of obtaining counsel and support for the accused. Charles Wheaton headed it up.[20]

Outside of Syracuse, abolitionists throughout the North praised the town for its successful resistance to the execution of the Fugitive Slave Law. Although Liberty Party men had been the primary movers in planning the rescue, the Garrisonian abolitionists of Boston were particularly effusive in their praise. Their own Samuel J. May was given much credit for the event, and they gloried in the city's defiance of the federal government. Antislavery meetings held in Rhode Island, New Jersey, Boston, and Philadelphia expressed their approval in speeches and resolutions, and one New York paper called May "a national treasure."[21] An article in the *Liberator* said that "the fires of liberty have not clean gone out in Western New York," and it praised Syracuse citizens who had "acquitted themselves like men."[22]

Garrisonian Henry C. Wright wrote from Boston to James Haughton, a colleague in Ireland. When he heard of the Syracuse rescue, he said, "I was just wild with joy and thanksgiving." Wright saw the act as a rejection of the power of the federal government, and he declared: "The slavery question is being settled. The work of Revolution is going on."[23]

The rescue was not the end of the resistance in Syracuse. Abolitionists intended to use the court system to make further gains in their agitation against the law, not only in the defense that would be provided for the rescuers but also through a complaint made against Jerry's "kidnappers." The first arrest that took place in Syracuse, in fact, was not of one of the rescuers, but was of James Lear, Jerry's claimant. On Wheaton's complaint, Police Justice House arrested him on October 2. Soon after, he arrested Federal Marshal Allen. Both men were charged with violating a New York personal liberty law passed in 1840, which was known as "An Act to Extend the Right of Trial by Jury." Ellen Wheaton wrote in her diary of their indictments before an Onondaga Grand Jury and of her husband's role in initiating the charges. Prosecution under the state law, she said, "will present matters in a new light, indeed." She didn't know what the reaction would be in Washington, DC, but she was certain that "they will be exceedingly mad against us."[24] Lear returned to Missouri and he died in late 1852, and so he was never tried by the state of New York. Allen, however, was slated to face a New York jury in February 1852. The citizens of Syracuse and the abolitionists of the Northern states eagerly awaited his trial. It would be yet another vehicle with which they could protest the hated Fugitive Slave Law. "This idea of an Onondaga grand jury indicting marshals for their efforts to execute a law of Congress," said an editorial in *Frederick Douglass' Paper*, "is alike novel and genius."[25]

Before Allen had to face judgment, however, the pending indictments of the rescuers absorbed everyone's attention. Around 150 Syracuse residents took advantage of the reduced railroad tickets to Auburn, traveling there to provide moral support during the hearing, which took place October 15–18. Charles Wheaton was among them, and he reported in a letter to Gerrit Smith that the atmosphere of the city was "joyful." He expressed satisfaction that "Freedom's battle is waging hotter and hotter."[26]

Although some resented the removal of the hearing from Syracuse to Auburn, abolitionists were heartened by the news that Judge Alfred Conkling would preside over the proceedings. He had ruled against slave catchers before; perhaps he would be friendly to the Jerry rescuers. Gerrit Smith wrote to Conkling on October 17 urging that he could play an important role in the fight to end slavery by deciding that the rescuers were not guilty of treason. He pressed Conkling to have the "discernment and the bravery to lead the way in this revolution."[27]

At the hearing, Conkling did not align himself closely with the abolitionists. "He gave us fanatics some hot shots," Wheaton reported to Smith.[28] Conkling, however, also did not support the motion to indict the defendants for treason. After Lawrence presented his case at Auburn, Conkling's decision was that there was "no evidence of previous combination and arming for the purpose of 'levying war against the United States'" on the part of the accused. He deemed that treason charges, therefore, were inappropriate. Instead, he found that the defendants had "aided, abetted and assisted" Jerry in his escape from Marshal Allen, which was a violation of Section 7 of the Fugitive Slave Law. He instructed the defendants to appear at the U.S. District Court in Buffalo in November, where a formal indictment hearing would take place before a grand jury.[29] Conkling set bail for all the defendants: $2000 for the white rescuers and $500 for the black rescuers. Charles Wheaton and Samuel J. May were both among the signers of the bail bonds. Wheaton wrote to Smith that "we had plenty of volunteers for the bonds for all, Black and White."[30]

The first person who signed for bail was Senator William Seward. Auburn was his home town, and he had attended the hearing in order to support the rescuers. According to Wheaton's account to Smith, Seward had "rather begged the privilege of signing all the bonds, which he did."[31] As he signed, Seward turned to District Attorney Lawrence, and "playfully" asked him "whether signing the bond would be considered constructive treason." When court was adjourned, Seward invited all of the defendants and visitors from Syracuse to his home "where they enjoyed a half hour in friendly chat and introductions to the Honorable Senator, a man admired and beloved because of his unyielding advocacy of Liberty."[32]

The Buffalo grand jury met to hear the rescue cases at the beginning of November, and all of the men held over by Conkling at the Auburn hearing were indicted. Additional arrests had taken place in the interim, and included an additional black defendant, Enoch Reed, as well as white Syracuse residents William Crandall, L. H. Salisbury, J. B. Brigham, and Montgomery Merrick, bringing the total of indictments to thirteen. All gave bail in Buffalo and were ordered to appear for trial before the U.S. District Court at Albany in January 1852.

• • •

Meanwhile, as abolitionists and other Northerners who opposed the Fugitive Slave Law praised the rescue and rallied around those who were arrested, others throughout the nation criticized the Syracuse resistance to the Fugitive Slave Law. Throughout the state of New York, newspapers of diverse affiliations referenced the rescue and its aftermath with the following: "The Outrage at Syracuse" (*Albany Express*), "Crime and Treason" (*Rochester Democrat*), "Progress of Traitors at Syracuse" (*Rochester Advertiser*), and "The Mob at Syracuse" (*Oneida Whig*). Criticism came from both the major political parties. The *Albany Argus*, the state's most influential Democratic paper, wrote of the events surrounding the rescue: "They are a reproach to the city where they are permitted, a burning disgrace to the State at large." It criticized the "armed mob" of Syracuse for its attempt "to overcome a judicial tribunal by violence, to trample on the law." The New York Whig Convention in November 1851 denounced the Syracuse "demagogues who proclaimed the Constitution an atrocious bargain."[33] The rescue was big news outside of the state as well. The *Washington Union* called for the government to declare that the city was in a "state of siege," to occupy the city with the army, and to declare it "out of the Union until it repented of its sins."[34]

There was also, of course, criticism of the rescue in the Southern states. In Jerry's former home of Hannibal, Missouri, the rescue was of special local interest. Editor Orion Clemens reported on the rescue in the *Hannibal Journal and Union*. Aiding him at the newspaper was Orion's brother Samuel—who would later gain fame for work produced under his pen name, Mark Twain. Clemens's treatment shows the frustration that Southern men felt at Northern refusals to abide by the Fugitive Slave Law. Noting the trouble that James Lear had encountered with the required paperwork for Jerry's rendition, their article warned that "people should be more careful about making out such documents" and speculated that the "trouble" in New York might have been avoided if there had not been the delay in Jerry's arrest. Despite this conclusion about the paperwork, Clemens laid the blame for the rescue on the town of Syracuse and the "disposition prevailing the entire community, hostile to extending to Southern men rights guaranteed to them by the Constitution and the laws of the land." Although not everyone in the city was involved in the rescue, he concluded that it would not have occurred "if the respectable men who did not appear among the ruffians, had not patted them on the shoulder, and secretly winked at their proceedings." The article concluded that "slaveholders may now set it down as an established fact, that their chance of recovering a fugitive slave is almost as good in Canada, a foreign country, as in the Northern States of this Union. . . . The slaveholder may calculate on recovering his lost property, in those States, if at all, at the imminent risk of failure, after incurring heavy expense, and at the hazard of his life."[35]

The rescue caught the attention of journalists in other parts of the South as well. Accounts were reprinted from Northern newspapers for Southern audiences, and the editorial comments that accompanied them blamed the rescue on Northern free blacks and abolitionists. *The Savannah Daily Morning News* made such a claim, saying that the burgeoning free black population was "a festering sore upon the body politic." Virginia's *Raleigh Register* expressed a similar opinion, and it called for the Northern states to exclude the settlement of free blacks within their borders. The *Fayetteville Observer*, a paper in North Carolina, complained that the newspapers of the city along with "a Reverend Mr. May" had been "printing and preaching against the Fugitive Slave Law and urging its nullification." The mob action on October 1, it said, was "the natural consequence of such teachings." Southern papers also demanded that the terms of the Compromise of 1850 be upheld. *The Fayetteville Observer* proclaimed that those that participated in the rescue should be "arrested as traitors, tried as traitors, and hanged as traitors." The *Raleigh Register* reminded the nation of the Georgia Platform with an announcement that if the North did not punish those who refused to submit to the terms of the Fugitive Slave Law, then the Southern states would leave the Union.[36]

In Syracuse much of the popular opinion supported the rescuers. "From my limited opportunities of judging," Ellen Wheaton wrote in her diary entry for October 15, "it seems the whole community are agitated concerning this matter,—and a large number, if not the majority, are on the side of right."[37] There were, however, some town members who criticized the town's act of resistance on October 1: the Law and Order crowd, made up mostly of conservative Whigs who had a year before urged support for the Compromise of 1850 for the sake of Union and had encouraged Webster to visit the city in May 1851.

The *Syracuse Star* once again was the journalistic vehicle used by the Law and Order advocates to further their cause. On October 3, the paper proclaimed that the town had been "disgraced" and lamented that Syracuse had become a "matter of notoriety in every state and every city of the Union." The *Star* was critical of not only the rescuers but also public officials who had failed to prevent Jerry's escape. In the immediate aftermath of the rescue, Charles Wheaton and Origen Vandenburgh were targeted for their roles in disbanding the militia units, and Charles's brother Horace, the "Free Democrat" mayor of the city, was accused of dismissing the need to keep peace in the city.[38]

The *Star*, however, blamed the rescue primarily on the abolitionists, and it went to great pains to define the act as one perpetrated by "fanatics" and not by the general population of Syracuse. In late October and early November, the *Star* printed a series of open letters exchanged between Samuel J. May, who it considered to be one of the most dangerous of the "fanatics," and two correspondents who condemned the rescue. Both accused May of encouraging an act that could bring about disunion and civil war. In one of his letters, May responded: "It is no more fair in you to charge me with desiring to plunge my country into the horrors of servile and civil war, than it would be to charge that I was eager to be engulfed in the ocean, because I have said that I would rather be drowned than burned to death." He wrote that although he abhorred war he would support one that led to the end of slavery, pointing out that the celebrated

American Revolutionary War was fought over lesser slights than those suffered by the American slave.[39]

Opposition to the rescue was also expressed outside of the *Syracuse Star*. The Law and Order contingent circulated a petition condemning the rescue. They were able to collect 668 signatures.[40] In addition, the Law and Order men held a meeting on October 25 in order to condemn the rescue and assert their city's respect for federal law. The reputation of Syracuse "can be vindicated only by an open and bold repudiation of the deed which obscures it," they announced.[41] There was some disorder at the meeting, as supporters of the rescuers attended and tried to influence the proceedings. Several men were forcibly removed from the meeting hall. The *Syracuse Standard* reported that the meeting "began in tumult, continued in an uproar, and ended in confusion." A Syracuse correspondent to the *New York Tribune* characterized the meeting as "a specimen of mobocracy and violence . . . decidedly superior to the mob engaged in the rescue of Jerry."[42]

Despite the disorder, the meeting to censure the rescue continued. Syracuse attorney Harvey Baldwin asserted that the American Union depended on Syracuse denouncing the act of October 1. James Brooks, a writer for the *New York Express*, said that the town of Syracuse was dependent on the federal government and should make a show of respect for its authority. If members of the town did not repudiate the rescue, he said, they were liable to lose the twenty percent duty on foreign salt that helped to keep the Syracuse salt industry so healthy. Another Syracuse lawyer, S. D. Dillaye, reiterated the *Star's* argument that the abolitionists, and not the citizens of Syracuse, were to blame for the rescue. After the speeches, the meeting passed resolutions that expressed regret for the rescue, proclaimed that the town upheld the Constitution and the laws of the United States, and blamed the abolitionist "preachers of sedition" for the rescue of Jerry.[43]

• • •

While the Law and Order crowd promoted acquiescence to federal law, supporters of the rescuers remained busy. On November 20, the Syracuse Vigilance Committee arranged for a second "County Rally for Freedom" in City Hall. There, Charles Wheaton presented a series of resolutions that condemned the Fugitive Slave Law of 1850 as a violation of the Northern states' rights. The resolutions asserted that the Constitution did not sanction slavery and that it gave the federal government no authority over the institution. Slavery was a state matter, and therefore, Wheaton announced, "we propose a direct appeal to the State of New York in its *sovereign capacity*, against the further occupancy of its busy streets and fair fields" of slave catchers. They called for New York citizens to "flood the tables of the Legislature" with petitions asking for the state to pledge itself "to secure and maintain the complete protection and rights of every human being who sets foot on our soil."

Wheaton also announced the formation of an "Executive Committee for the Cause of Freedom in the State of New York." Its job would be to promote agitation against the Fugitive Slave Law "through the voice of the living speaker, papers, periodicals and tracts, and generally by all such means as wisdom and experience would suggest." It would collect funds, organize conventions, and set up committees of correspondence to encourage resistance to the hated law.

The last act of the meeting was the approval of an "Address from the Freemen of Onondaga." In it, they laid out their case against the Fugitive Slave Law, and stated that they would not obey it. The officers of the meeting then sent a copy of both the address and the minutes of their meeting to President Fillmore and to the governors of the Northern states.[44]

As all of this was going on, Ellen Wheaton continued to worry about her husband, Charles. "I shall rejoice if this affair comes to a quiet termination and we can once more settle down into a peaceful way of life," Ellen wrote. She missed her husband, who was taken up with the events surrounding the rescue's aftermath. Even "when he is present in body," she said, "he is most of the time absent in spirit,— which is very trying to me." In the face of hardship, she said, "I hope I shall have patience to endure, and so may we all, the trials put upon us, and conduct ourselves with cheerfulness and fortitude."[45]

CHAPTER 12

Trials

Caroline Loguen had much in common with Ellen Wheaton. She too had a house full of children under her care: four, with another on the way, at the time of the Jerry Rescue. She too found herself shouldering a heavy burden at home while her husband traveled about speaking against slavery. If the passage of the Fugitive Slave Law had disrupted Ellen's life, however, it had completely transformed Caroline's. In addition to providing care for her children, Caroline also took responsibility for the fugitives that took refuge in her home at 293 East Genesee Street, which served as the central Underground Railroad depot of Syracuse. The numbers who came to stay in the windowless fugitive chamber she and her husband had built into their brown-shingled two-story house multiplied after Congress passed the Fugitive Slave Law. Care for them became a full-time job for Caroline. And even more than Ellen, Caroline found the events surrounding the Jerry Rescue a source of much anxiety, for her husband Jermain faced not only the possibility of arrest for defiance of the Fugitive Slave Law, but there was also the chance that slave catchers might attempt to seize him and return him to Tennessee.

• • •

After the rescue, several witnesses accused Jermain Loguen of assaulting a federal marshal and encouraging the violence of others. Loguen admitted to his presence at the planning of the rescue, but he denied that he had participated in the storming of the building or had committed any type of violence. Because the charges made against

Caroline Loguen.
From the Collection of the Onondaga Historical Association, 321 Montgomery Street, Syracuse, NY 13202

him were false, he was unconcerned about facing trial for his role in the rescue, but he and Caroline were fearful about the possibility that, if detained, Loguen might be returned to slavery. Caroline urged Jermain to take refuge in Canada to avoid arrest, at least until the excitement following the rescue abated.[1]

Loguen complied. He followed the Underground Railroad route that he had sent others along, traveling first to the nearby town of Skaneateles, then to Rochester, and finally crossing the international border into Canada. He stayed in the Canadian village of St. Catharines for seven months, where he preached at a local black church and aided other fugitives who had fled from the United States. The *Syracuse Standard* announced on October 6 that Loguen had left the city. "The cheeks of every American should burn with shame that such a man is compelled to fly to a monarchical government to preserve his liberty," it proclaimed.[2]

After he arrived in St. Catharines, Loguen wrote a letter to District Attorney Lawrence denying the charges that had been made against him. He had heard that Lawrence had contacted the Canadian government to try to arrange for his extradition, and he wished to address that action. "Indeed, Mr. Lawrence," he wrote, "were I not assured that your ulterior object is to re-enslave me, most willing would I, upon American soil, meet the charges and refute the sworn—falsely sworn—allegations of the miserable creatures of the government against me." He told Lawrence that he was sure that the Canadian government would not cooperate with him: "Thank God, sir, no Fillmore, nor Webster, nor any other such men, has to do with public officers in this really free country."[3]

Loguen also wrote a letter to the New York governor, Washington Hunt, reiterating his willingness to face trial for the rescue if he could be assured that he would be safe from slave catchers. He had committed no crime, he told him, and only fled to maintain his liberty. "I was born unconstitutionally," he wrote. "It was my misfortune, not my fault," he said to him, "that I was born in the South, contrary to the Declaration of Independence." Would the governor protect him from the slave catcher? Loguen never received an answer.[4]

In January 1852, Loguen wrote to John Thomas: "I suppose the trials of those noble men who are charged with the rescue of Jerry are in progress at Albany the present week." He said that he wished he stood with them: "I trust it will not be long till the reign of pro-slavery terror will explode and I shall have the unspeakable happiness of returning to my family, to dwell with them securely, even if perils have to be encountered in the attempt."[5]

The trials of the rescuers had indeed commenced in Albany in January 1852, but little came of them. They were postponed to June, and in June they were postponed to October, and in October they were postponed to January 1853. In January 1853, black defendant Enoch Reed was tried. He was found "not guilty" of violating the Fugitive Slave Law, since it had never been determined that John McReynolds, who had purchased Jerry *in absentia*, had a valid claim to Jerry's service under the law. Instead Reed was found guilty of resisting a federal officer. Reed appealed the case, but he died before it could be heard.

The hearings stretched out to the end of the year, by which time the government had held eight general and special sessions to consider the Jerry Rescue cases. In the trials of other rescuers, the government had even less luck than it had with Reed. William Salmon was acquitted. Hung juries produced mistrials in the cases of Ira Cobb and J. B. Brigham. The other cases were indefinitely postponed. The hearings ceased at the end of 1853, but the government did not officially drop the charges against the remaining defendants until June 1861.

Although none were officially punished for the rescue, the trials were a great hardship to the accused. A writer for the *New York Tribune* commented on this, complaining in October 1853 that the defendants had always been ready for trial, but the government had "subjected them to the expense of going from term to term" with constant delays. The thinking of government officials, it speculated, was "Good enough for them, punish them in that way if you cannot any other."[6]

In February 1852, as Jermain Loguen languished in Canadian exile and as the trials of the rescuers were just gearing up, the state of New York held its own trial, pursuing the charges that the abolitionists had brought against Marshal Allen for violating a state personal liberty law. Gerrit Smith, appearing as special counsel for the prosecution, would present the case against Allen, turning the trial into a vehicle for arguing against the constitutionality of the Fugitive Slave Law. As Don E. Fehrenbacher has pointed out, the Fugitive Slave Law involved jurisdictional disputes between the state and federal governments as well as sectional arguments about slavery and individual rights.[7] The case against Allen is a perfect example of this. Smith and his colleagues pressed for the supremacy of a New York personal liberty law over the federal Fugitive Slave Law. "Let us thank God that there are state, as well as national tribunals, and that it does not follow, because the latter are in the hands of slaveholders, the former are also," Smith said when he addressed a Liberty Party meeting after the rescue. "Let us thank God, that, if we can be murdered by federal courts, kidnappers can be punished by State courts."[8]

Smith also used the proceedings against Allen to argue against the constitutionality of the Fugitive Slave Law. He hinged much of his case for its unconstitutionality on the fact that it did not provide a trial by jury for the accused, but he also emphasized the Liberty Party's argument that slavery itself was unconstitutional. The Founding Fathers had not intended to protect slavery in perpetuity, he said, nor had they intended that the federal government be made "a gigantic slave-catcher."

Smith pressed that the Fugitive Slave Law should be deemed unconstitutional because it denied the natural rights of man, and he pointed out that as a federal official, Allen had sworn to uphold "not an Act of Congress, but the Constitution." Since the law was unconstitutional, then "neither judge nor marshal can obey it with impunity."[9]

The abolitionists had little hope of winning the case against Allen, but they pursued it anyway as a vehicle for drawing further attention to their arguments against the validity of the Fugitive Slave Law. In the end, the judge, R. P. Marvin, instructed the jury to find Allen "not guilty" because he had been executing a federal law. "The presumption is generally in favor of the Constitutionality of a law," Marvin said, "and the onus of showing that it is not Constitutional, is upon him who attacks it." He did not believe that the prosecution had done so.[10]

· · ·

After the Allen case concluded but before any of the rescuers were tried, Loguen decided to take his chances and return to Syracuse. He was heartened by a reassuring editorial that John Thomas had published in *Frederick Douglass' Paper*, which had argued that Loguen would be as safe there as he would be in Canada. "The people can hardly keep hands off from J. R. Lawrence now," Thomas wrote, "Should he arrest, or attempt to arrest Loguen as a slave, he would at last be compelled to pull up stakes and move to the South. The people would not endure such a wretch."[11] In late spring, Loguen made his way home, despite his failure to receive any assurances that he would not be prey for the slave catcher. He hoped that Thomas' speculation about Syracuse was correct.

Within months of Loguen's return, the town rose to Thomas's expectations. In October 1852, Loguen took a trip to nearby Skaneateles during which he found himself on the same train as Marshal Allen and two police officers. When Loguen exited the train at his stop, so did the officers. Several passengers aboard the train witnessed this, and when they arrived at the railroad depot in Auburn, they telegraphed a message to abolitionist friends in Syracuse, informing them that Loguen had been arrested.

The Syracuse Vigilance Committee went to work. The bells of the Congregational Church tolled the signal that a fugitive was in danger, and a great crowd gathered in order to mobilize in Loguen's behalf. After the crowd assembled, however, the next train arrived in Syracuse with Marshal Allen aboard. When he learned of the rumor about Loguen, the marshal addressed the crowd, announcing that there had been no arrest. He explained that he had been coincidentally on the same train as Loguen because he had been subpoenaed to testify at hearing at the circuit court in Auburn. He held no warrant for Loguen, he said, and he had no intention of arresting him. He explained that the police officers who had exited the train behind Loguen near Skaneateles had been in pursuit of a "nest of thieves," one of whom was detained at the railroad junction.[12]

After he returned to Syracuse, Loguen resumed his duties as pastor of People's A.M.E. Zion Church in Syracuse, but he spent a great amount of his time traveling through upstate New York, speaking out against the Fugitive Slave Law and collecting money for the Underground Railroad. He also kept up a vigorous correspondence with abolitionists in Great Britain, who sent money to support his efforts. When he was home, he and his family spent most of their time attending to their duties as Underground Railroad operatives.

In the aftermath of the Jerry Rescue, Loguen and others conducted the Underground Railroad in Syracuse in a very public manner. They printed announcements about fugitives passing through Syracuse in the town's newspapers. Loguen advertised his address at 293 East Genesee Street as an Underground Railway station, and he furnished monthly and yearly reports of the number of travelers that came through his home.[13] After the Jerry Rescue, then, the Underground Railroad was no longer "under ground" in the openly defiant town of Syracuse. It was out in the open. Such was the confidence of Loguen and his fellow abolitionists that the Fugitive Slave Law had been effectively nullified in their town; it had become a place where a fugitive slave printed his address in the local paper, inviting other fugitives into his home.

In 1855, Loguen resigned from his ministry at the A.M.E. Zion church for several years in order to pursue his Underground Railroad work full-time. Loguen's interest in fugitive aid went far beyond providing a place for escaping slaves to stay on their journey to freedom. He helped to secure jobs for those who wished to stay in New York, and he conducted marriage ceremonies for former slaves who wanted a religious service to formalize their bonds with one another. In 1856 he helped to establish a home for fugitives in Canada, and he went on a tour of Canadian freedmen's communities in order to assess their condition and encourage aid for their support. In addition, he continued his antislavery lectures throughout New York.

While Loguen worked full-time on his Underground Railroad activities, he was dependent on donations to provide for his family and the fugitives that came through his home. In 1856, Samuel J. May organized a Fugitive Slave Aid Society in Syracuse to raise money and supplies for Loguen's efforts. Just a year later, however, May dissolved the organization, placing the Underground Railroad operation of the city wholly in Loguen's hands. He explained his action saying that Loguen "having been a slave and a fugitive himself knows best how to provide for that class of sufferers."[14] After this point all donations would go directly to the Loguen home. Thus in Syracuse there emerged a racial division of labor in the operation of the Underground Railroad. While white citizens provided money and moral support for fugitive aid, it was Syracuse's black community, headed up by Loguen, who took fugitives into their homes and cared for them on a personal level.

As Jermain Loguen dedicated himself to fugitive aid, his wife helped him, spending most of her time taking care of her busy household. In many ways Caroline was the quintessential minister's wife, whose job it is to support her husband's ministry. This she did, but because her husband's efforts were so expansive, so too were hers. Although Loguen was known as the "stationmaster" for the Underground Railroad in Syracuse, he was often away from his "station." He traveled frequently to give antislavery lectures, assess the conditions of Canadian freedmen, and minister to other communities.

During this time, Caroline stayed busy, making sure that the refuge that was her home ran smoothly. Samuel J. May, who was close to the Loguen family, recognized Caroline's crucial role in Syracuse noting that fugitives "came at any time of day or night, and often in numbers which it was difficult for her to accommodate, or to provide for elsewhere," but she always received them. "They came, too, not unfrequently, in such conditions of destitution and uncleanness, as subjected her to the most disagreeable inconvenience," he said, "but she rendered efficiently the services that were needed, and spared no pains to get the fugitives into places of safety and self support."[15]

Although she stayed busy, Caroline's activities were not enough to distract her from the anxiety that overcame her during the periods when her husband was away from home. She and her family were always aware of Jermain's vulnerability under the Fugitive Slave Law. Slave catchers could at any time arrest him and bring him back to Tennessee. The Loguens felt that Jermain was reasonably secure in Syracuse, but there was no guarantee of safety when he was out on the open road. Despite these fears, Loguen continued to travel, and he continued to reject the option of purchasing his own freedom.

In February 1860, Loguen made it clear that he would never do so. That month, Loguen received a letter from Tennessee addressed to "Jarm Logue." In it Sarah Logue, the widow of his former owner Mannasseth, informed Loguen that her family was experiencing hard economic times. She told him that their troubles were "partly in consequence of your running away and stealing Old Rock, our fine mare." The family had sold twelve acres of land as well as Loguen's brother and sister, Abe and Ann, in order to make ends meet. She wrote to ask Loguen for money so that she could reclaim her land. If he would send her one thousand dollars, she told him, "I will give up all claim on you." If he did not send money, she threatened, "I will sell you to some one else, and you may rest assured that the time is not far distant when things will be changed with you."[16]

Loguen wrote a curt reply to Tennessee, berating Mrs. Logue for the sale of his family: "You have the unutterable meanness to ask me to return and be your miserable chattel, or in lieu thereof send you $1000 to enable you to redeem the land, but not to redeem my poor brother and sister!" He said that he would never purchase his freedom. If he were even to consider it, it would be to save his siblings from going "off into sugar and cotton fields, to be kicked, and cuffed, and whipped, and to groan and die" and not to save her land. "If you or any other speculator on my body and rights, wish to know how I regard my rights," he wrote, "they need but come here and lay their hands on me to enslave me." Loguen asserted that they would not be able to take him. "I stand among a free people, who, I thank God, sympathize with my rights, and the rights of mankind." He told her that "my strong and brave friends, in this city and State, will be my rescuers and avengers" should she send someone after him.[17] He would be safe in Syracuse.

CHAPTER 13

....

The Jerry Level

In October 1853, just two years after Jerry's flight across the U.S.–Canadian border to Kingston, Ontario, the town's newspapers announced the famous fugitive's death. On October 10 he had succumbed to tuberculosis. A week later the *Syracuse Standard* published a poem to honor Jerry's memory:

> ... He has gone to a land where human enactments,
>   However oppressive or stringent they be,
> Will meet with no Marshal to force their exactments,
>   No bevy of hell-hounds to shackle the free. . . .[1]

During the two years after his escape to Canada, news about Jerry had trickled into Syracuse, primarily through Edward Wheeler, a Syracuse man who had moved to Kingston in 1852 in order to run a saw mill. Wheeler knew Jerry and had participated in his rescue. After arriving in Kingston, he had found Jerry working for a chair manufacturer downtown, and the two became reacquainted. Jerry, in fact, expressed his gratitude to Wheeler by making the Wheeler family a chair for their home. That chair, according to Wheeler's son, was a cherished heirloom to his family members, who always referred to it as the "Jerry Chair." In 1922 the Wheeler family gifted it to the Onondaga Historical Association, where it is now housed.[2] Jerry also crafted a hickory cane with a deer's horn for a handle, and he had Wheeler, on one of his visits to Syracuse, deliver it to Charles Wheaton to thank him for the role he played in his deliverance.[3]

Chair made by Jerry and presented to Edward Wheeler to thank him for his role in his rescue. The "Jerry Chair" is now held by the Onondaga Historical Association. *From the Collection of the Onondaga Historical Association, 321 Montgomery Street, Syracuse, NY 13202*

Wheeler was the one who reported Jerry's death to the Syracuse press. He sent a letter to the *Syracuse Standard* informing Syracusans that Jerry "has gone to meet his original master, and perhaps father, where all are on an equality." He gave news of Jerry's life in Kingston. Jerry had resumed his trade of coopering, and a year before he had attended an evangelical revival where he had been "converted." Wheeler assured Syracuse residents that "his conduct has been quite good as that of the generality of men of his rank in life." He commented that although Jerry "had occasional fits of despondency and loneliness, . . . he was generally cheerful and contented with his lot."[4] Jerry was buried under the name "William Henry" in the unmarked "common ground" of Cataraqui Cemetery in Kingston.[5]

Even as the life of Jerry the man ended, the life of Jerry the symbol was just beginning. In Syracuse and beyond, his name became synonymous with the plight of the fugitive, and his rescue with efforts to resist the Fugitive Slave Law. Antislavery men and women in central New York quipped, "He knows which way Jerry went," to refer to supporters of their cause.[6] Abolitionists referred to slaves in need of aid as "Jerrys."[7] Gerrit Smith, in speeches before antislavery audiences, repeatedly summoned his listeners to "come up to the Jerry level," by acknowledging "that right, and right only, is law."[8]

• • •

The memory of Jerry, and of his rescue, was deliberately kept alive in order to nurture continued resistance to the Fugitive Slave Law and encourage sympathy for the plight of the slave. One year after the rescue took place, the Jerry Rescue Committee organized a celebration of the anniversary of the event. New York antislavery men would continue to honor "Jerry Rescue Day" until the eve of the Civil War. For almost a decade it served as an abolitionist holiday.

The invitation to the first celebration announced the committee's intentions. "It is fitting that the 1st of October should be made a Festival Day in the Calendar of Freedom," it said, "so long as in America is denied to one innocent human being the exercise of those Rights which are the free gift of the Almighty Father of us all."[9] Around five thousand men and women, black and white, attended the first commemoration of the Jerry Rescue. At the proceedings, the New York political abolitionists and the Garrisonians, including William Lloyd Garrison himself, came together. Gerrit Smith presided.

They heard speeches, read poetry, sang songs, and passed resolutions that upheld the right to resist laws for slavery. They collected funds to defray the legal expenses of the rescuers and to keep the Underground Railroad running in central New York. They characterized the rescue of Jerry as "of incalculable value, as an efficient teacher and practical expounder of sound doctrines in regard to law, and slavery, and kidnapping," and pledged that it "should be celebrated every year, until there shall no longer be a wretch, who dares to be a kidnapper, and no longer be a slaveholder to give employment to a kidnapper."[10]

A year later, enthusiasm about the rescue's legacy remained high, and the Jerry Rescue celebration was on its way to becoming an important tradition in the town of Syracuse. The Jerry Rescue Committee once again invited Gerrit Smith to preside over the celebration of the events of October 1, 1851, which was, they declared "a day on which a community practically asserted and sanctioned the declarations of

'76," and that in their view was "much holier than the 4th of July, 1776."[11] Smith agreed to preside, and his chairmanship of the proceedings became a tradition through the 1850s. The revolutionary rhetoric also became a tradition. The committee's public invitation to the third anniversary celebration likened the rescue's impact to that of the Boston Tea Party and claimed that it had been "animated by that faith which was taught by the fathers of the American Revolution, 'that resistance to tyrants is obedience to God.'"[12]

Although many in Syracuse enthusiastically celebrated the rescue each year, there were those who worried about the message imparted by the city's celebration of an act that defied federal law. Early on, Syracuse officials attempted to impede the Jerry Rescue Day celebrations. At the first anniversary event, the Syracuse Common Council denied the use of City Hall and encouraged Syracuse residents not to attend. Antislavery men attributed the reluctance of Syracuse officials to celebrate the rescue to the position taken by the Whig and Democratic parties on the Fugitive Slave Law; both had in 1852 included in their party platforms endorsements of the Compromise of 1850. Party leaders wanted the slavery issue out of politics, and they wanted Americans in both the North and South to consider the terms of the compromise the final adjustment of the slavery question.[13]

While elected officials toed the party line, John Wilkinson, owner of the Syracuse Railroad, saved the day. He offered up his unfinished engine house, a 150-foot rotunda capable of holding up to 10,000 people, for the proceedings. Despite fears that the Law and Order crowd might protest the event, the celebration was held without disruption.[14]

City officials eventually became more accommodating. In 1853, there was once again an attempt to deny facilities to hold the Jerry Rescue Day celebration, but the mayor overruled the council, and City Hall was opened up for the second anniversary proceedings.[15] The abolitionists were able to procure facilities for all the future commemorations of the rescue.

The first Jerry Rescue Day celebrations brought together abolitionists and antislavery men of all stripes, including Garrisonians, Liberty Party members, and Free Soilers. In time, however, the anniversary of the rescue became a venue for debating the issues that divided the various antislavery factions. Old discussions about the legitimacy of political action and the question of nonresistance arose at the annual event as abolitionists considered the significance of the rescue.

Perhaps the most divisive issue following the rescue was that of violent resistance to American law. Although most abolitionists had traditionally eschewed the use of force in their agitation against American slavery, after the passage of the Fugitive Slave Law opinions had begun to shift. In New York, many black and some white abolitionists sanctioned defensive violence in order to protect the "hunted slave," and after the Jerry Rescue these men promoted the idea of forcible resistance to slave law with increasing boldness. Frederick Douglass was the primary spokesman for the use of forcible resistance at the Jerry Rescue Day events. In 1853 he engaged in an argument with Garrisonian William Burleigh on the subject, and at the 1854 celebration he and Garrison himself held a lengthy debate. After Garrison spoke, pressing for an emphasis on moral suasion in the fight against slavery, Douglass lifted up a pair of broken shackles, said to be those that held Jerry, and he asked "how many arguments, frowns, resolutions, appeals, and entreaties would be necessary to break them."[16]

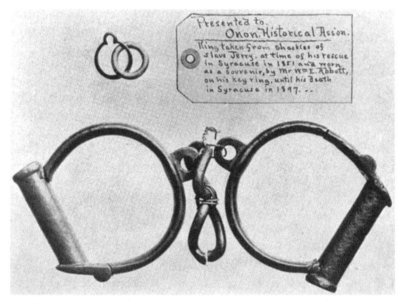

The shackles that bound Jerry, now held by the Onondaga Historical Association.
From the Collection of the Onondaga Historical Association, 321 Montgomery Street, Syracuse, NY 13202

As the rhetoric of the Jerry Rescue Day celebrations became more forceful and as speakers increasingly sanctioned defensive violence, Garrisonian abolitionists became more critical of the proceedings. Their arguments played out in the press. In the *Liberator*, Garrison issued a sharp rebuke to the New York abolitionists who had rejected the ideal of nonresistance. Writers from *Frederick Douglass' Paper* defended the use of force. One editorial in the latter gloried that "in the light and heat" of the resistance of the Jerry Rescuers, "how is that other, the non-resistant spirit, melting down, and the delusion vanishing away!" Because of the willingness to use force to defy the Fugitive Slave Law, fugitives were safe in Syracuse.[17]

In the midst of this debate, Gerrit Smith wrote to Garrison and expressed hope that the two factions of abolitionists would continue to honor the memory of the rescue together. "Jerry was rescued on the grounds that there is, and can be, no law for slavery," he said. On that point both factions agreed.[18]

Tensions nevertheless grew. The debates about nonresistance alienated Garrison and many of his Boston colleagues, but regional loyalties also did their part to divide the abolitionists. At the Jerry Rescue celebrations, participants habitually lauded the city of Syracuse as an exceptional place, where no fugitive could be taken. This was all fine, but the New York abolitionists were also in the habit of comparing the safety of Syracuse with the insecurity of Boston regarding fugitive slaves. At the first rescue celebration, Gerrit Smith referenced the return of Thomas Sims to slavery from Boston. "Now which was right, Boston or Syracuse?" Smith asked the crowd. He called Sims' return to slavery the "heaviest blow ever struck against American liberty," and Jerry's rescue the "heaviest blow ever struck at American slavery."[19]

In 1854, yet another failed attempt to rescue a fugitive from kidnappers in Boston heightened these tensions. Anthony Burns, who had fled to the city from slavery in Virginia, was taken by authorities in May of that year. Boston antislavery forces mobilized to liberate Burns, following much the same pattern as had taken place in Syracuse in 1851. During the Burns rendition hearing, a mob formed outside the courthouse building. Antislavery forces called a public meeting, and that evening a biracial group of men stormed the courthouse. Here the similarities end, however. Not only did the attempted rescue fail, but during the course of it one of Burns's guards was fatally wounded. Real violence had taken place, and the federal government quickly dispatched troops to Boston to keep order, effectively placing the city under martial law. As in the Sims case of three years before, Burns was ordered back into slavery, and federal troops—this time several thousand of them—lined the streets of Boston as guards escorted the fugitive through the city to board a boat that would transport him back to Virginia.[20] The Burns excitement infected the 1854 celebration of the Jerry Rescue and led to inevitable comparisons between the two rescue attempts. Garrison responded to them by asserting that Syracuse was not, in fact, a free city as its proponents claimed. If it were, they would not have had to send Jerry on to Canada for refuge. "Why did you not keep Jerry and defend him here?" he asked the Syracuse celebrants.[21]

The battle between New York and Boston continued to haunt the Jerry Rescue Day celebrations. In 1855, Garrison refused to attend, arguing that the event had become a Liberty Party affair, used to promote Gerrit Smith's agenda. Garrison's critique was not unfounded. Smith had indeed been using the celebrations to promote political abolition, calling upon Northern citizens to come up to the "Jerry Level" in their voting habits. The "Jerry Level" had become his pet term for the recognition that there was a "Higher Law" than those of the nation—that government actions that violated God's laws were not legitimate. Although Smith believed that Garrison and his crowd were at the "Jerry Level" in their complete rejection of American slave law, Smith argued that their rejection of political action negated their ability to fight such law effectively.[22]

The escalation of sectional politics in the United States also affected the tone of the Jerry Rescue celebrations. In 1854, Senator Stephen Douglas introduced the Kansas Nebraska Bill to Congress. This bill, proposed by the man who had helped to foster the passage of the Compromise of 1850, undid previous sectional settlements. In organizing the new territories of Kansas and Nebraska, Douglas proposed that their policies concerning slavery be decided by the people of the territories. This opened up the possibility of slavery in a region that had previously been designated free territory by the terms of the Missouri Compromise. Many Northerners felt betrayed. With every accommodation to slavery, it seemed that they were asked in later years to concede even more to the slave power. Complaints about slaveholder dominance of the federal government grew louder.

In 1854, anger at both the Kansas Nebraska Bill and the return of Anthony Burns to slavery helped to renew Northern protests of the Fugitive Slave Law. Resistance to the law had actually quieted somewhat following the Jerry Rescue, as in 1852 and 1853 both political parties worked to calm the sectional crisis. After the events of 1854, however, many Northerners who previously had urged obedience to the Fugitive Slave Law as part of a permanent adjustment of sectional issues abandoned this position and joined in with those who opposed the slave power. In Syracuse and elsewhere throughout the North, "Anti-Nebraska" meetings were held to protest the proposed repudiation of the Missouri Compromise. The Free Soil movement grew after the Kansas Nebraska Bill became law and eventually culminated in the rise of the Republican Party.

The Kansas Nebraska Act affected the general rhetoric of the Jerry Rescue celebrations. In 1854, the Jerry Rescue Committee called upon men and women of all religious and political persuasions "who would redeem our Republic from the dominion of a most unscrupulous oligarchy of Slaveholders" to celebrate the third anniversary of the rescue.[23] The meeting, according to the *Syracuse Standard*, was "crowded almost to suffocation" and participants combined discussion of the legacy of the rescue "together with a number of sarcastic hits at the Nebraska Bill and its author."[24]

In 1855, the sectional settlement deteriorated further. As a result of the Kansas Nebraska Act, violence had broken out between proslavery and antislavery settlers in Kansas as each faction competed for influence over the territorial position on slavery. This led to the extended debate on the appropriateness of violent resistance that took place at the celebration of the fourth anniversary of the Jerry Rescue. It also led to even more resentment of the slave power, and the rhetoric of the celebration fused the question of slavery in the territories with the question of slave law in the supposedly free Northern states. "How clearly in the light of the Fugitive Act, the Nebraska Act, the still more astounding attempt to compel slavery in Kansas, does the slave power declare that the only issue it will accept is the legality of slavery anywhere and everywhere," the invitation to the event complained.[25]

The situation in Kansas continued to influence the Jerry Rescue anniversary in 1856. "Bleeding Kansas" had become a drawn-out affair, and violence entered into the halls of Congress when South Carolina representative Preston Brooks struck Massachusetts senator Charles Sumner repeatedly with a cane due to insulting remarks he made about his uncle, Senator Andrew Butler, during a speech on "The Crime against Kansas." Everywhere one looked, the question of American slavery was shrouded in violence.[26]

Accordingly, the rhetoric sanctioning forcible resistance escalated at the Jerry Rescue celebration of 1856. The invitation to the fifth anniversary proceedings called for the attendance of "all who will strike for freedom when freedom demands it . . . who will meet force with force to that end, either the enemy be armed with the forms of law, or, as in Kansas, marches without a mask upon our constitutions, laws and liberties." It was important to commemorate the rescue, the Jerry Rescue Committee asserted, proclaiming that "the bold blow that rescued Jerry anticipated the impudent aggressions of each successive year, until freemen have no alternative, but to use the bayonet and other weapons as slavery uses them to kill the enemy or be killed by them."[27]

• • •

The discussions about violent resistance to slave law never entirely subsided, but at each Jerry Rescue Day celebration, Gerrit Smith, presiding over the event, brought the focus back to his pleas for Americans to come up the "Jerry Level" by supporting no church, political party, or law that sanctioned slavery. At the 1857 celebration, Smith said that "the Jerry of today is the Christ of today," and he addressed all Christians: "If you do not see Him in every poor Jerry, and feel a faith that impels you to help rescue him, then your belief in Jesus Christ is but superstition or hypocrisy." He held a similar position regarding political parties. "Until American slavery is abolished," he said, "a resolution endorsing the rescue of Jerry should be brought to every political meeting in the land." He argued that if a party's leaders refused to support the resolution, then the party had failed to reach the "Jerry Level" and should not be supported.[28]

CHAPTER 14

....

Sectional Crisis

. . .

The Jerry Rescue Day celebrations continued in the aftermath of the Kansas Nebraska Act, but as the nation became increasingly divided over the expansion of slavery in the late 1850s, Gerrit Smith found that more and more antislavery men fell from the "Jerry Level." At the 1857 celebration, Smith expressed his concern about the growth of the Republican Party, which had sprung out of the Anti-Nebraska movement. The new party claimed to be a "Friend of Freedom," Smith said, but he feared that by absorbing the abolitionist element and then dampening its purpose, the new Free Soil–oriented party was instead its "most deadly enemy."[1]

• • •

The Republican Party consisted of a coalition of disaffected Northern Whigs and Democrats, Free Soilers, and abolitionists; and its focus was on the way that the slave power infringed upon white rights. As was true of its predecessor the Free Soil Party, the Republican Party's central goal was to block further expansion of slavery in the United States so that free labor could flourish, thus allowing upward mobility for white citizens who emigrated into new territories. The plight of the slaves in the Southern states figured little into the Republican Party rhetoric, and party leaders did not attack slavery where it already existed. Also, while many members of the party wanted to repeal the Fugitive Slave Law, this goal did not become part of the Republican platform. By focusing primarily on the expansion of slavery, party leaders hoped to attract a broad swathe of Northern voters and accumulate enough political might to end the slave power's dominance over federal affairs. The nation then could move in the direction of establishing a modern economy based on free labor.[2] Abolitionists who joined with the Republicans indeed compromised their goals by pushing for something far less than universal emancipation, but they reasoned that the new party's platform would provide an entering wedge for bringing about the end of slavery at a later date.

As the Republican Party gained strength, Smith watched helplessly as more and more allies abandoned political abolitionism to join with the Republicans. He, Frederick Douglass, Jermain Loguen, and others had in 1855 formed a new party out of the remainder of the Liberty Party. They called themselves the Radical Abolition Party, and they continued to press for an end to slavery in all of the states as well as the territories. Their influence on national politics remained negligible, however, and Smith was frustrated. Whether or not the Republican Party and others who expressed a limited form of antislavery "can or cannot contribute somewhat to the downfall of slavery," Smith said, a "bloodless, peaceful end will never be reached until the friends of freedom shall have mounted 'the Jerry level,' and branded the whole system of American slavery as a piracy and outlaw."[3]

By 1859, Smith had had enough. John Thomas, that year's chair of the Jerry Rescue Committee, wrote to him with an invitation to take his usual position at the head of the annual celebration. Smith refused. On August 27, 1859, from his home in Peterboro, he wrote a letter to Thomas explaining why he did not wish to participate in the celebration of the eighth anniversary of the Jerry Rescue. Smith said he still considered the rescue "a great and glorious event" that announced to the federal government that "there was no law and could be no law for slavery." In recent years, however, he felt that the celebration had degenerated into a "grand annual hypocrisy." Although the sentiments of each Jerry Rescue celebration remained true, Smith complained that "the vast majority of those who enjoyed the anniversaries returned home to act with the proslavery parties in church and state." He recommended that the Syracuse men give up the Jerry Rescue celebration. Because it was disingenuous, he said, "the cause of freedom is disgraced and hindered, instead of being honored and promoted by it."

After he urged the end of the rescue celebrations, Smith issued a warning. Because Americans had failed to lift themselves up to the "Jerry Level" in politics, he believed that it was "perhaps too late to bring slavery to an end by peaceable means—too late to vote it down." He blamed the Republican Party for this turn of events. Not only did it leave slavery intact in the South, but it "lifts not a finger to repeal the Fugitive Slave Act; nor to abolish slavery in the District of Columbia; nor to abolish the interstate traffic in human flesh." More than that, the Republican Party had done little to prevent the slave power's increasing hold over the federal government. Since the party's rise, the Dred Scott decision had come down from the Supreme Court, and it had effectively declared that slavery could not be barred from any part of the United States. "Slavery," Smith said, "has never strengthened itself so rapidly as during the existence of this new and misnamed Republican Party." He finished his letter to Thomas with a final, eerie warning. Because black men had reached the "conclusion that no resource is left to them but in God and insurrections," Smith said, "for insurrections, then, we may look any year, any month, any day."[4]

• • •

Six weeks later, abolitionist John Brown led his raid on the federal arsenal at Harper's Ferry, Virginia. Brown, a radical reformer who had traveled in New York abolitionist circles, led twenty-two white and black men into Virginia. Their goal: to spark a slave insurrection. They planned to seize weapons from the arsenal, arm nearby slaves, and begin an uprising against slavery. Brown failed to fulfill this mission, but the raid was nevertheless a significant act, for it would help bring sectional tensions to a breaking point. After the raid was quashed by federal troops and Brown and his allies were killed or arrested, Southerners expressed outrage that abolitionist agitators had invaded Southern soil, attacked a federal facility, and attempted to stir up a slave rebellion. In the North, there was a divided reaction to the raid. Some, including the Republican Party leadership, condemned Brown, but many celebrated him. After Brown was hanged for murder and treason, throughout the North many declared him to be an antislavery martyr.

Gerrit Smith was implicated in John Brown's raid. He was his longtime associate and had met with Brown and a number of his supporters at his Peterboro home before the raid. He also had provided him with funds. Northern and Southern papers reprinted Smith's letter to John Thomas that had predicted a violent uprising. One commented that it "very curiously foreshadowed" the event.[5] Jermain Loguen and Frederick Douglass also were associates of Brown. Both had met with him on occasions to discuss his plans in Virginia, but neither participated in the actual raid. Even so, the connections between the political abolitionists of New York and John Brown reveal their sense of frustration. The vast majority of Northern men had refused to come up to the "Jerry Level" in their voting habits. Perhaps only violent rebellion would bring the end of slavery after all.[6]

The annual celebration of the Jerry Rescue continued without Smith, but only for one additional year. The last Jerry Rescue Day to be held before the Civil War was in October 1860, a month before Republican candidate Abraham Lincoln won the presidency and less than three months before the Southern states began seceding from the Union. In the absence of Smith, Beriah Green, Samuel J. May, and Frederick Douglass spoke at the proceedings.

Those who gathered passed familiar resolutions against the Fugitive Slave Law, declaring that it was illegitimate. They praised other slave rescues that had occurred in the years since Jerry was liberated in Syracuse. They issued a resolution declaring that the inflamed Southern reactions to John Brown's raid in the South "attest the felt guilt, the fearful exposures and perils of slavery." The violent rhetoric of previous celebrations, however, had been toned down. Republican Party man Charles Sumner, who in 1859 returned to the Senate after a long recovery following the Preston Brooks attack, wrote a letter to Samuel J. May to be read at the celebration. Sumner expressed his own abhorrence of the Fugitive Slave Law, calling it "a flagrant violation of the Constitution and of the most cherished human rights," but he called for "the honorable, freedom-loving, peaceful, good and law-abiding citizens" to attack the law through "an aroused Public Opinion" and "without violence of any kind."[7]

Although Sumner and some other Republicans—including William Seward who had assumed a position of leadership within the new party—expressed their dislike of the Fugitive Slave Law, opposition to it never became part of the Republican Party platform. Abraham Lincoln was against bringing such opposition into the Republican agenda even though he also found its terms repugnant. He took much the same position on the law that Daniel Webster, deceased since October 1852, had held. He argued that the law did not violate the Constitution; it was passed legally, and it should be respected as part of a compromise that would help preserve the Union.[8] The resolutions passed at the 1860 Jerry Rescue Day nevertheless remained uncompromising. Because of the looming sectional crisis, members of the meeting proclaimed: "We feel impelled to urge anew and with fresh emphasis, immediate and unconditional emancipation, always a duty, and now become a stern, instant necessity."[9]

Despite Lincoln's attempt at moderation and despite the limits of Republican Party goals, the election of a Republican president nevertheless sparked secession. Southerners did not believe that slavery was safe in a nation that had elected a Northern candidate who was hostile in any way to their cherished institution. The contest over slavery in the territories and the Republican Party's ascendance in federal politics were thus the proximate causes of secession and Civil War.

Northern reactions to the Fugitive Slave Law, such as that which had occurred in Syracuse, nevertheless played an important role in creating the sectional discord that led to the extreme Southern reaction to Lincoln's election. Passed as part of a compromise meant to preserve the Union, the law instead widened the sectional breach. It moved many Northerners toward the position taken by abolitionists who argued that slavery corrupted the nation and interfered with white as well as black liberties. Northern resistance to the law then provoked outrage among Southerners who resented the Northern refusals to follow federal laws that protected slavery.

Comments from a North Carolina newspaper illustrate the Southern position with a mention of the Jerry Rescue. In reply to the Republican Party's assertion that it would not interfere with slavery in the states, it said: "Has there been such a non-interference? Have such necessary and feasible steps been taken? The history of the last ten years, from the Jerry rescue down to the Harper's Ferry invasion, is full of disproof of such assumptions. . . . What then? We do not need to answer the question. It will, we imagine, soon be answered, disastrously for both sections, unexpectedly perhaps to the North."[10] When the Southern states seceded from the Union, they listed abolitionist agitation and Northern refusals to follow the Fugitive Slave Law among its grievances. Somewhat ironically, the refusal of Northern states to surrender to a federal law coexisted with Southern assertions of their own states' rights concerning slavery in the secession ordinances that justified disunion.[11]

By the end of the 1850s, more abolitionists also believed that disunion and war loomed, but of course they had a different perspective on the cause of the crisis. Jermain Loguen's autobiography, published in 1859, ends with the prophecy: "The coldness with which the politics and religion of this country turn away from the slave, is sad but irresistible proof that slavery must go down in blood."[12]

....

Conclusion

The Jerry Rescue did not cause the Civil War, but the story of
the rescue does provide a lens for understanding some of the
nuances of the American sectional crisis. In particular, it illustrates the way in which the Fugitive Slave Law of 1850 contributed
to the breach between the North and the South. The law triggered an
explosion of resentment throughout the North. It energized various
factions of abolitionists and provoked debates about the appropriate
way to resist the law and protect fugitives. It sparked fear in the hearts
of Northern blacks and led to an increase in Underground Railroad
activity throughout the nation as men and women vulnerable to the
law made their way further North to avoid arrest and enslavement. It
also created such outrage that many Northerners who had previously
been ambivalent about the slavery issue (or had, in fact, supported the
right of Southerners to own slaves) came to resent the Southern slave
power and support efforts to limit its reach.

One of the most interesting elements of the rescue story is what it
reveals about the issue of "states' rights" in antebellum politics. An understanding of the debates over the Fugitive Slave Law reverses the usual
conceptions about the role this ideology played in the coming of the Civil
War. In their protests, Northerners who opposed the Fugitive Slave
Law complained about the privileging of federal over state law and about
the way in which the federal government interfered with one's individual
rights. Conversely, Southern leaders insisted on active federal protection
of the rights of slave owners within the boundaries of free states. The
Jerry Rescue and other stories of Northern resistance to the Fugitive
Slave Law force those who insist that the Civil War was primarily about
Southern states' rights to look at the sectional conflict in a new way.

161

The Jerry Rescue story also reveals important issues that the abolitionists faced, such as whether or not to condone violent resistance and whether to work within the political system or outside of it. Various factions of abolitionists—Liberty Party men, Garrisonians, and leaders of the black community—all debated the merits of the rescue within the larger context of how to attack the institution of American slavery. Indeed, the issues sparked by the rescue are larger than the abolitionist movement itself. Most reform movements face the same kinds of questions. A discussion of the dilemmas that abolitionists faced regarding their means of protest and of the various techniques that they used in order to facilitate their opposition to the law lends itself to the consideration of the broader issues of civil disobedience and how to deal with government policies that one considers immoral.

Additionally, the story of Jerry's rescue highlights the prominent role that African Americans played in resisting the law. Many historians have argued that slaves helped to emancipate themselves during the Civil War by running away to Union lines. One may argue that fugitives also played an important role in bringing about the war that ultimately ended slavery. The events in Syracuse help to illustrate this role, and they reveal the way that race figured into resistance to the law. While blacks worked together with white abolitionists to protest the law, they often agitated in different ways. Black leaders tended to resist the law in more forceful and direct ways while prominent white abolitionists aided the black community with legal aid, money, and rhetoric. The centrality of the black community's actions in both the rescue of Jerry and the implementation of Underground Railroad activities in Syracuse reveals how those who had the most to lose—their freedom—rose against the Fugitive Slave Law and inspired sympathetic whites to join with them.

Finally, while the Jerry Rescue story deserves attention because of the way it sheds light on issues important to the American sectional crisis, the Jerry Rescue story also remains an important event in the local history of Syracuse. With the rescue, antislavery citizens in Syracuse effectively nullified a federal law that they found immoral, turning their city into political Free Soil. Although the desire to cordon Syracuse off as a place of refuge never went uncontested in the city, those who wished to stand against the federal slave catching bureaucracy succeeded in their goal of blocking the enforcement of a federal law in their town. Jerry had been freed, and after the rescue no other fugitive was able to be taken within its boundaries.

FOR FURTHER READING

....

The literature on the American sectional crisis is vast, and so the suggestions included here barely scratch the surface of the scholarship that will be interesting and useful to those who wish to delve into further study of the subjects touched upon in this book. My intention in this section is to provide readers with a good starting place for their intellectual journey as well as to tip my hat to the works that most directly informed the preceding narrative.

For primary source material on the Jerry Rescue and on the Syracuse antislavery movement, the Onondaga Historical Association is a treasure trove. There, researchers can find a well-organized collection of both primary and secondary materials on those topics. Most of the primary documents referred to in this work were found in that association's collections. Supplementary material can be found in online databases like the *Black Abolitionist Papers* (Proquest) and *19th Century U.S. Newspapers* (Gale-Cengage Learning). In addition, the Boston Public Library holds important papers on the abolitionist movement, and much of the correspondence of Samuel J. May is available there. Syracuse University's Special Collections holds the papers of Gerrit Smith, another important actor in the preceding narrative.

I relied heavily on autobiographies published by several of the abolitionists who were involved in the Syracuse events. These include Jermain Loguen, *The Rev. J. W. Loguen as a Slave and a Free Man* (New York: Negro Universities Press, 1968); Samuel J. May, *Some*

Recollections of Our Antislavery Conflict (Boston: Fields, Osgood, & Co., 1869); and Samuel Ringgold Ward, *Autobiography of a Fugitive Negro* (New York: Arno Press, 1968). The *Diary of Ellen Birdseye Wheaton* (Boston: Privately Published, 1923) provides a valuable woman's perspective on the antislavery movement in Syracuse.

In addition to these primary sources, biographies are available for a number of the important actors in the book. Those I consulted include Donald Yacovone, *Samuel Joseph May and the Dilemmas of the Liberal Persuasion* (Philadelphia: Temple University Press, 1991); Carol M. Hunter, *To Set the Captives Free: Reverend Jermain Wesley Loguen and the Struggle for Freedom in Central New York* (New York: Arno Press, 1993); Ronald K. Burke, *Samuel Ringgold Ward: Christian Abolitionist* (New York: Garland Publishing, 1995); Norman K. Dann, *Practical Dreamer: Gerrit Smith and the Crusade for Social Reform* (Hamilton, NY: Log Cabin Books, 2009); Walter Stahr, *Seward: Lincoln's Indispensable Man* (New York: Simon & Schuster, 2012); and Robert Remini, *Daniel Webster: The Man and His Time* (New York: W. W. Norton and Co., 1997). An unpublished biography of Jermain and Caroline Loguen's daughter Sarah Loguen Fraser, written by her own daughter, provides insight into the Loguen family's home life and Underground Railroad activities. Interestingly Sarah became one of the country's first black female doctors. See Gregoria Fraser Goins, *Miss Doc*, in Box 36-4, Folders 51–52, of the Goins Papers in the Manuscript Division of the Moorland-Spingarn Research Center, Howard University.

Although this is the first book-length treatment of the Jerry Rescue, there have been several journal articles on the subject. Among these are W. Freeman Galpin, "The Jerry Rescue," in *New York History* 26:1 (1945); Jayme A. Sokolow, "The Jerry McHenry Rescue and the Growth of Northern Antislavery Sentiment during the 1850s" in *American Studies* 16:3 (December 1982); Monique Patenaude Roach, "The Rescue of William 'Jerry' Henry: Antislavery and Racism in the Burned-over District" in *New York History* 82:2 (Spring 2001); and Angela Murphy, "'It Outlaws Me, and I Outlaw it!': Resistance to the Fugitive Slave Law in Syracuse, New York" in *Afro-Americans in New York Life and History* 28:1 (2004). Accounts of the rescue are also available in the form of speeches that were given at twentieth-century celebrations of Jerry Rescue Day in Syracuse. These are available at the Onondaga Historical Association. One of the most useful addresses, given by Earl F. Sperry, was published by the society along with numerous eyewitness accounts of the rescue. See Franklin H. Chase (ed.), *The Jerry Rescue, October 1, 1851* (Syracuse: Onondaga Historical Association, 1924). An interesting fictionalized account of the Syracuse rescue is a novel by Constance Robertson, *Fire Bell in the Night* (Philadelphia: The Blakiston Company, 1944).

For a good overview of the abolition movement, see James Brewer Stewart, *Holy Warriors: The Abolitionists and American Slavery* (New York: Hill and Wang, 1995). On political abolitionism and the Liberty Party see Richard H. Sewell, *Ballots for Freedom: Antislavery Politics in the United States* (New York: W. W. Norton and Co., 1980) and Reinhard O. Johnson, *The Liberty Party 1840–1848: Antislavery Third-Party Politics in the United States* (Baton Rouge: LSU Press, 2009). Studies that highlight abolitionist activity in upstate New York are Douglas M. Strong, *Perfectionist Politics: Abolitionism and the Religious Tensions of American Democracy* (Syracuse: Syracuse University Press, 1999); John Stauffer, *The Black Hearts of Men: Radical Abolitionists and the Transformation of Race* (Cambridge: Harvard University Press, 2002); Gerald Sorin, *The New York Abolitionists: A Case Study of Political Radicalism* (Westport, CT: Greenwood Press, 1971); and Milton C. Sernett, *North Star Country: Upstate New York and the Crusade for African American Freedom* (Syracuse: Syracuse University Press, 2002). Sernett's book provides an especially valuable overview of antislavery and Underground Railroad activity in the area around Syracuse.

There are many books that deal with the American sectional crisis. Good, concise overviews include Bruce Levine, *Half Slave and Half Free: The Roots of the Civil War* (New York: Hill and Wang, 2005); Michael F. Holt, *The Political Crisis of the 1850s* (New York: W. W. Norton and Co., 1983); and Eric Walther, *The Shattering of the Union: America in the 1850s* (Lanham, MD: Rowman and Littlefield, 2003). More expansive accounts that have had particular influence on my thinking are Richard J. Carwardine, *Evangelicals and Politics in Antebellum America* (Knoxville: University of Tennessee Press, 1997); Don E. Fehrenbacher, *The Slaveholding Republic: An Account of the United States Government's Relations to Slavery* (New York: Oxford University Press, 2001); David M. Potter, *The Impending Crisis: America Before the Civil War* (New York: Harper, 1976);

and Elizabeth R. Varon, *Disunion! The Coming of the American Civil War 1789–1859* (Chapel Hill: University of North Carolina Press, 2008). A highly readable book that deals specifically with the debates over the Compromise of 1850 is Fergus M. Bordewich, *America's Great Debate: Henry Clay, Stephen A. Douglas, and the Compromise that Preserved the Union* (New York: Simon & Schuster, 2012). Also revealing are Paul Finkelman's numerous works that deal with slavery in American jurisprudence and politics. Among these are *Slavery and the Founders: Race and Liberty in the Age of Jefferson* (New York: M. E. Sharpe, 2001).

For information on the Underground Railroad one should consult the following classic treatments: William Still, *The Underground Railroad: Authentic Narratives and First-Hand Accounts* (Mineola, NY: Dover Publications, 2007); Wilbur H. Siebert, *The Underground Railroad from Slavery to Freedom: A Comprehensive History* (London: The Macmillan Company, 1898); and Larry Gara, *The Liberty Line: The Legend of the Underground Railroad* (Lexington: University Press of Kentucky, 1961). More recent works on the subject include Jacqueline L. Tobin, *From Midnight to Dawn: The Last Tracks of the Underground Railroad* (New York: Anchor Books, 2007); Fergus M. Bordewich, *Bound for Canaan: The Epic Story of the Underground Railroad, America's First Civil Rights Movement* (New York: Amistad, 2005); and R. J. M. Blackett, *Making Freedom: The Underground Railroad and the Politics of Slavery* (Chapel Hill: University of North Carolina Press, 2013). For a regional study of New York and New Jersey see William J. Switala, *Underground Railroad in New York and New Jersey* (Mechanicsburg, PA: Stackpole Books, 2006).

A classic book on the impact of the Fugitive Slave Law of 1850 is Stanley W. Campbell, *The Slave Catchers: Enforcement of the Fugitive Slave Law, 1850–1860* (Chapel Hill: University of North Carolina Press, 1968). More recent treatments of the subject include Steven Lubet, *Fugitive Justice: Runaways, Rescuers, and Slavery on Trial* (Cambridge, MA: Belknap Press, 2010); and Gordon S. Barker, *Fugitive Slaves and the Unfinished American Revolution: Eight Cases, 1848–1856* (New York: McFarland, 2013). Stanley Harrold's *Border War: Fighting Slavery before the Civil War* (Chapel Hill: University of North Carolina Press, 2010) emphasizes the importance of the fugitive slave issue in the border regions between the Northern and Southern states. David G. Smith's *On the*

Edge of Freedom: The Fugitive Slave Issue in South Central Pennsylvania, 1820–1870 (New York: Fordham University Press, 2012) focuses on the impact of fugitive slave policy in a more specific region. Finally, those who are interested in reading other studies that deal with specific episodes of resistance to the Fugitive Slave Law in the Northern states should consult the following: Gary Collison, *Shadrach Minkins: From Fugitive Slave to Citizen* (Cambridge: Harvard University Press, 1997); H. Robert Baker, *The Rescue of Joshua Glover: A Fugitive Slave, the Constitution, and the Coming of the Civil War* (Athens, OH: Ohio University Press, 2006); Thomas P. Slaughter, *Bloody Dawn: The Christiana Riot and Racial Violence in the Antebellum North* (New York: Oxford University Press, 1991); Scott Christianson, *Freeing Charles: The Struggle to Free a Slave on the Eve of the Civil War* (Urbana: University of Illinois Press, 2010); Nat Brandt, *The Town that Started the Civil War* (New York: Dell Publishing, 1990); Nat Brandt and Yanna Kroyt Brandt, *In the Shadow of the Civil War: Passmore Williamson and the Rescue of Jane Johnson* (Columbia: University of South Carolina Press, 2007); Albert J. von Frank, *The Trials of Anthony Burns: Freedom and Slavery in Emerson's Boston* (Cambridge: Harvard University Press, 1998); and Earl M. Maltz, *Fugitive Slave on Trial: The Anthony Burns Case and Abolitionist Outrage* (Lawrence: University Press of Kansas, 2010).

ENDNOTES

Introduction

1. Jerry's arrest for petit larceny is recorded in Board of Supervisors Account #184, City of Syracuse. See also arrest reports for assault on Sarah Colwell in the *Syracuse Standard*, December 24, 1850, February 19, 1851, March 25, 1851. All of the above are in the Jerry Rescue Collection, Biographical Information Folder, Onondaga County Historical Association, Syracuse, NY (hereafter cited as OHA). On June 22, 1852, the *Standard* reported that Sarah Colwell pressed the same charges against another man, Anthony Brooks.

2. According to the *Syracuse Standard*, October 2, 1851, Jerry was told he was to be charged "with some slight offence." Later, on January 28, 1853, it reported that he was told he was detained because "those women up town" had made complaints against him again. Another account claims that he was informed that his arrest was for theft. See Jermain Wesley Loguen, *The Rev. J. W. Loguen, As a Slave and As a Freeman: A Narrative of Real Life* (New York: Negro Universities Press, 1968), 400. See also discussion of these accounts in Carol M. Hunter, *To Set the Captives Free: Reverend Jermain Wesley Loguen and the Struggle for Freedom in Central New York* (New York: Arno Press, 1993), 144, n.44.

3. For general accounts of Jerry's arrest under the Fugitive Slave Law, see *Syracuse Standard*, October 8, 1851; *Frederick Douglass' Paper*, October 9, 1851; U.S. Circuit Court, Special Term, Albany, January 26, 1853, in *Frederick Douglass' Paper*, February 4 and 11, 1853; Earl E. Sperry,

The Jerry Rescue (Syracuse, OHA, 1924), 41; W. Freeman Galpin, "The Jerry Rescue," *New York History* 26:1 (January 1945), 22–25.

4. Loguen, *The Rev. J. W. Loguen*, 399.

5. Samuel J. May, *Some Recollections of Our Antislavery Conflict* (Boston: Fields, Osgood & Co., 1869), 375.

6. *Frederick Douglass' Paper*, October 9, 1851.

Chapter 1

1. Hunter, *To Set the Captives Free*, 112.

2. No one knows for sure how many fugitives escaped to the North during the antebellum period, but most historians estimate that it was between one and two thousand a year, a very small percentage of the total number of slaves.

3. "Former Mayor C. F. Williston's Recollections" in *The Jerry Rescue*, ed. Franklin H. Chase (Syracuse: OHA, 1924), 29–30.

4. *Syracuse Standard*, December 4, 1852, August 10, 1853, April 15, 1854.

5. See, for example, *Syracuse Standard*, May 17, 1850, October 10, 1855, and July 29, 1856. For more on the experiences of free Northern blacks see Leon F. Litwack, *North of Slavery: The Negro in the Free States, 1790–1860* (Chicago: University of Chicago Press, 1965).

6. Samuel Ringgold Ward, *Autobiography of a Fugitive Negro* (Chicago: Johnson Publishing Company, 1970), 118; Loguen, *The Rev. J. W. Loguen*, 401.

7. For an overview of slavery in Missouri see Diane Mutti Burke, *On Slavery's Border: Missouri's Small-Slaveholding Households* (Athens: University of Georgia Press, 2010).

8. For discussions of the Southern slave economy see James L. Huston, *Calculating the Value of the Union: Slavery, Property Rights, and the Economic Origins of the Civil War* (Chapel Hill: University of North Carolina Press, 2003); Lacy K. Ford, *Deliver Us from Evil: The Slavery Question in the Old South* (New York: Oxford University Press, 2009); Walter Johnson, *River of Dark Dreams: Slavery and Empire in the Cotton Kingdom* (Cambridge: Belknap Press, 2013).

9. Jerry is listed as "William Henry" in Syracuse arrest records, the Syracuse city directory, and in his death records. His friends and acquaintances in Syracuse all referred to him as Jerry. He also was called "Jerry" by his family when he was enslaved in Missouri. See "Testimony of Joshua Gentry, U.S. Circuit Court, Special Term,

Albany, February 1, 1853," in *Frederick Douglass' Paper*, February 18, 1853.

10. Ibid.

11. For books on sectionalism in the early republic, see Robert Pierce Forbes, *The Missouri Compromise and Its Aftermath: Slavery and the Meaning of America* (Chapel Hill: University of North Carolina Press, 2007); John Craig Hammond, *Slavery, Freedom, and Expansion in the Early American West* (Charlottesville: University of Virginia Press, 2007); Matthew Mason, *Slavery and Politics in the Early American Republic* (Chapel Hill: University of North Carolina Press, 2006).

12. Terrell Dempsey, *Searching for Jim: Slavery in Sam Clemens's World* (Columbia: University of Missouri Press, 2003), 8.

13. Thomas Jefferson to John Holmes, April 22, 1820.

Chapter 2

1. Testimony of Joshua Gentry, February 1, 1853.

2. Testimony of John McReynolds, U.S. Circuit Court, Special Term, Albany, February 1, 1853, in *Frederick Douglass' Paper*, February 18, 1853.

3. Testimony of Joshua Gentry, February 1, 1853.

4. On slave flight, see R. J. M. Blackett, "Dispossessing Massa: Fugitive Slaves and the Politics of Slavery after 1850," *American Nineteenth Century History* 102 (June 2009), 119–136; John Hope Franklin and Loren Schweninger, *Runaway Slaves: Rebels on the Plantation* (New York: Oxford University Press, 1999).

5. "James Madison's Notes" in *1787: Drafting the U.S. Constitution*, Vol. II, ed. Wilbourn Benton (College Station: Texas A&M University Press, 1986), 1377–9.

6. On slavery in New York, see A. Judd Northrup, *Slavery in New York: A Historical Sketch* (Albany: University of the State of New York: 1900); Ira Berlin and Leslie M. Harris, eds., *Slavery in New York* (New York: The New Press, 2005). On emancipation in New York, see David N. Gellman, *Emancipating New York: The Politics of Slavery and Freedom 1777–1827* (Baton Rouge: Louisiana State University Press, 2006).

7. Capel Lofft, *Reports of Cases Adjudged in the Court of King's Bench, from Eastern Term 12 Geo.3. to Michaelmas 14 Geo.3.* (Dublin, 1790), 19. For further discussion of the impact of the case in the United States see Jerome Nadelhaft, 'The Somersett Case and Slavery: Myth,

Reality, and Repercussions," *Journal of Negro History* 51:3 (July 1966), 193–208.

8. "The Fugitive Slave Act, 1793," in *Encyclopedia of Emancipation and Abolition in the Transatlantic World*, v. 3, ed. Junius Rodriguez, (Armonk, NY: Sharpe Reference), 678.

9. Don E. Fehrenbacher, *The Slaveholding Republic: An Account of the United States Government's Relations to Slavery* (New York: Oxford University Press, 2001), 212.

10. "An Act to Prevent the Kidnapping of Free People of Color," April 1, 1808, in *Laws of the State of New York*, v. 30 (Albany: Webster and Skinner, 1809), 300. For more on personal liberty laws see Thomas D. Morris, *Free Men All: The Personal Liberty Laws of the North, 1780–1861* (Baltimore: Johns Hopkins University Press, 1974).

11. Steven Lubet, *Fugitive Justice: Runaways, Rescuers, and Slavery on Trial* (Cambridge: Belknap Press, 2010), 25.

12. *Prigg v. Pennsylvania*, 41 U.S. 539, 1842. For more on this case see Eric W. Plaag, "'Let the Constitution Perish': Prigg v. Pennsylvania, Joseph Story, and the Flawed Doctrine of Historical Necessity," *Slavery & Abolition* 25:3 (December 2004), 76–101; Robert Baker, *Prigg v. Pennsylvania: Slavery, the Supreme Court, and the Ambivalent Constitution* (Lawrence: University Press of Kansas, 2012).

13. For more on Seward and New York personal liberty laws, see Paul Finkelman, "The Protection of Black Rights in Seward's New York," *Civil War History* 34:3 (September 1988), 211–34.

14. On the Nullification Crisis, see William W. Freehling, *Prelude to Civil War: The Nullification Controversy in South Carolina, 1816–1836* (New York: Oxford University Press, 1992).

15. Galpin, "The Jerry Rescue," 23–4.

Chapter 3

1. "Mrs. Margaret Sabine's Reminiscences, 1897," in Chase, *The Jerry Rescue*, 40–41.

2. Testimony of Joseph F. Sabine, U.S. Circuit Court, Special Term, January 26, 1853 in *Frederick Douglass' Paper*, February 4, 1852.

3. James Lawrence Case Opening and Testimony of Joseph F. Sabine, U.S. Circuit Court, Special Term, January 26, 1853.

4. Ibid.

5. "Mrs. Margaret Sabine's Reminiscences, 1897."

6. On Henry Clay's attempt to forge a compromise after the Mexican War, see Robert V. Remini, *At the Edge of the Precipice: Henry Clay*

and the Compromise that Saved the Union (New York: Basic Books, 2010).

7. *Congressional Globe*, 31st Congress, 1st Session, January 29, 1850.
8. Ibid.
9. Ibid., February 5, 1850.

Chapter 4

1. Loguen, *The Rev. J. W. Loguen*, 399–401.
2. Accounts of the Harriet Powell Rescue include Loguen, *The Rev. J. W. Loguen*, 366–8; *Syracuse Post Standard*, March 30, 1924; "Gerrit Smith Reminiscences by Dr. Ernst Held," in Chase, *The Jerry Rescue*, 60–67.
3. "Harriet Powell Reward Poster," in Chase, *The Jerry Rescue*, 61.
4. Loguen, *The Rev. J. W. Loguen*, 365.
5. Ibid., 369.
6. Elizabeth Cady Stanton, *Eighty Years and More: Reminiscences, 1815–1897* (New York: T. Fisher Unwin, 1898), 62–3.
7. May, *Recollections*, 324.
8. On the Burned-Over District see Whitney R. Cross, *The Burned-Over District: The Social and Intellectual History of Enthusiastic Religion in Western New York, 1800–1850* (Ithaca: Cornell University Press, 1981).
9. On Gerrit Smith's background and his antislavery activities, see Gerald Sorin, *The New York Abolitionists: A Case Study of Political Radicalism* (Westport, CT: Greenwood Publishing Corp., 1971), 27–37. For a biography of Smith, see Norman K. Dann, *Practical Dreamer: Gerrit Smith and the Crusade for Social Reform* (Hamilton, NY: Log Cabin Books, 2009).
10. There are many books on the abolition movement. A concise treatment is James Brewer Stewart, *Holy Warriors: The Abolitionists and American Slavery* (New York: Hill and Wang, 1997).
11. "Speech of Mr. Gerrit Smith," in *Proceedings of the New York Anti-Slavery Convention, Held at Utica, October 21, and the New York Anti-Slavery Society at Peterboro, October 22, 1835* (Utica: Standard and Democrat, 1835), 21.
12. Gerrit Smith to Abraham Cox, November 12, 1835, quoted in Sorin, *The New York Abolitionists*, 32.
13. Gerrit Smith to "Friend of Man," April 4, 1838, quoted in Sorin, *The New York Abolitionists*, 33.
14. Sorin, *The New York Abolitionists*, 52.

Chapter 5

1. May, *Recollections*, 375.
2. An excellent biography of Samuel J. May is Donald Yacovone, *Samuel Joseph May and the Dilemmas of the Liberal Persuasion, 1797–1871* (Philadelphia: Temple University Press, 1991).
3. Samuel Joseph May, *What Do Unitarians Believe?* (Syracuse: Masters & Lee, 1865), 3.
4. May, *Recollections*, 321.
5. Loguen, *The Rev. J. W. Loguen*, 357.
6. *Onondaga Standard*, October 7, 1835.
7. Overviews of early antislavery activity in Syracuse include Esther C. Loucks, "The Anti-Slavery Movement in Syracuse from 1839–1851," master's thesis (Syracuse University, 1934); Donald Bluestone, "A Brief Study of Antislavery Activities in Syracuse" (unpublished manuscript, OHA, 1960). A good study of antislavery in upstate New York is Milton C. Sernett, *North Star Country: Upstate New York and the Crusade for African American Freedom* (Syracuse: Syracuse University Press, 2002).
8. May, *Recollections*, 329.
9. For a general illustrated history of Syracuse see Dennis J. Connors, *Crossroads in Time: An Illustrated History of Syracuse* (Syracuse: Syracuse University Press, 2009).
10. "Parish B. Johnson's Recollections" in Chase, *The Jerry Rescue*, 37–40.
11. Loucks, "The Anti-Slavery Movement in Syracuse," 26.
12. Loguen, *The Rev. J. W. Loguen*, 358–9; 64.
13. For more on Cassius Clay, See H. Edward Richardson, *Cassius Marcellus Clay: Firebrand of Freedom* (University Press of Kentucky: Lexington, 1996).
14. *Religious Recorder*, September 18, 1845.
15. Ibid.; *New York Tribune*, October 6, 1845.
16. *Syracuse Star*, June 13, 1846.
17. Yacovone, *Samuel Joseph May*, 129–42.
18. *Syracuse Standard*, January 8, 1850.
19. *Liberator*, February 1, 1850.
20. *Syracuse Standard*, January 17, 1850.
21. Ibid., January 16, 1850.
22. Ibid., May 16 and 17, 1850.
23. Ibid., May 17, 1850.

Chapter 6

1. On the Compromise of 1850 debates, see Fergus M. Bordewich, *America's Great Debate: Henry Clay, Stephen A. Douglas, and the Compromise That Preserved the Union* (New York: Simon & Schuster, 2012); John C. Waugh, *On the Brink of Civil War: The Compromise of 1850 and How It Changed the Course of American History* (New York: Rowman & Littlefield, 2003).
2. *Congressional Globe*, 31st Congress, 1st Session, February 12, 1850.
3. Ibid., March 4, 1850.
4. Daniel Webster to Peter Harvey, February 13, 1850, in *Writings and Speeches of Daniel Webster*, v. 16 (Boston: Little, Brown & Co., 1903), 532.
5. *Congressional Globe*, 31st Congress, 1st Session, March 7, 1850.
6. Ibid., March 11, 1850.
7. Ibid., May 21, 1850.
8. On the Southern Convention, see Thelma Jennings, *The Nashville Convention: Southern Movement for Unity, 1848–1850* (Memphis: Memphis State University Press, 1980).
9. *Georgia Telegraph*, December 17, 1850.
10. "Fugitive Slave Act, 1850," in *Encyclopedia of Emancipation and Abolition in the Transatlantic World*, v. 3, 712.

Chapter 7

1. Loguen, *The Rev. J. W. Loguen*, 387–8.
2. Ibid., 402.
3. Ibid., 403.
4. *Syracuse Standard*, October 3, 1851; *New York Tribune*, October 4, 1851.
5. Loguen, *The Rev. J. W. Loguen*, 403.
6. George A. Green affidavit in *Syracuse Standard*, October 17, 1851.
7. Loguen, *The Rev. J. W. Loguen*, 402–3.
8. An excellent biography of Jermain W. Loguen is Hunter, *To Set the Captives Free*.
9. Solomon Northup, *Twelve Years a Slave: Narrative of Solomon Northup, a Citizen of New-York, Kidnapped in Washington City in 1841, and Rescued in 1853*, ed. David Wilson (Auburn, NY: Derby and Miller, 1853). For more on kidnapping, see Carol Wilson, *Freedom at Risk: The Kidnapping of Free Blacks in America, 1780–1865* (Lexington: University Press of Kentucky, 2009).

10. Quoted in Fergus M. Bordewich, *Bound for Canaan: The Underground Railroad and the War for the Soul of America* (New York: Amistad, 2005), 411.

11. Loguen, *The Rev. J. W. Loguen*, 379.

12. Ibid., 380.

13. Ibid., 393.

14. "Speech by Samuel Ringgold Ward delivered at Faneuil Hall, Boston Massachusetts, March 25, 1850," in *The Black Abolitionist Papers*, vol. 4, ed. C. Peter Ripley, 51; *Frederick Douglass' Paper*, August 20, 1852; Parker quoted in Lubet, *Fugitive Justice*, 58.

15. *Syracuse Standard*, September 20, 1850. Members of the new Syracuse black vigilance committee included John C. Foster, a laborer; Thomas G. White, a boat builder; the pastor of the African Congregational Church, Reverend John Lyles; and two lay preachers from the A. M. E. Zion Church, Thomas G. White and John Thomas.

16. *Syracuse Standard*, September 27, 1850.

17. *North Star*, September 5, 1850.

18. Ibid.

19. *Liberator*, October 25, 1850.

20. *Syracuse Standard*, September 24 and October 7, 1850; *Syracuse Journal*, October 7, 1850; May, *Recollections*, 351.

21. Hunter, *To Set the Captives Free*, 115. The committee members were Jermain Loguen, Abner Bates, Charles A. Wheaton, Dr. Lyman Clary, Vivus W. Smith, Charles B. Sedgwick, Hiram Putnam, E. W. Leavenworth, George Barnes, P. H. Agan, John Wilkinson, Rev. R. R. Raymond, and John Thomas.

22. Loguen, *The Rev. J. W. Loguen*, 393–4.

23. *Liberator*, October 25, 1850.

24. "Account of Judge Holmes," in *Syracuse Journal*, June 9, 1894; *New York Tribune*, October 8, 1851; *Frederick Douglass' Paper*, October 9, 1851.

25. "E. A. Sheldon to his Brother George," in *Autobiography of Edward Austin Sheldon* (New York: Ives-Butler Co., 1911), 95–6.

26. *Liberator*, October 17, 1851.

Chapter 8

1. Ward, *Autobiography of a Fugitive Negro*, 83.

2. On Samuel Ringgold Ward, see Ronald K. Burke, *Samuel Ringgold Ward: Christian Abolitionist* (New York: Garland, 1995).

3. William Wells Brown, *The Black Man, His Antecedents, His Genius, and His Achievements* (New York: T. Hamilton, 1863), 284–5.
4. "Speech on the Fugitive Slave Bill," in Burke, *Samuel Ringgold Ward,* 137–40; *Liberator,* April 5, 1850.
5. *Liberator,* October 11, 1850; *Impartial Citizen,* October 5, 1850.
6. Ward, *Autobiography,* 83–4.
7. On the Christiana affair, see Thomas P. Slaughter, *Bloody Dawn: The Christiana Riot and Racial Violence in the Antebellum North* (New York: Oxford University Press, 1991).
8. Ward, *Autobiography,* 83–4.
9. Ibid., 85–9.
10. *Syracuse Standard,* October 24 and 28, 1850; *Syracuse Journal,* October 24, 1850; *Liberator,* November 1, 1850.
11. On the Crafts, see *Running a Thousand Miles for Freedom: The Escape of William and Ellen Craft from Slavery,* ed. R. J. M. Blackett (Baton Rouge: Louisiana State University Press, 1999).
12. On the Hamlet affair, see Lewis Tappan, *The Fugitive Slave Bill: Its History and Unconstitutionality, with an Account of the Seizure and Enslavement of James Hamlet, and His Subsequent Restoration to Liberty* (New York: William Harned, 1850).
13. Stanley W. Campbell, *The Slave Catchers: Enforcement of the Fugitive Slave Law, 1850–1860* (Chapel Hill: University of North Carolina Press, 1968), 147.
14. On the Minkins rescue, see Gary Collison, *Shadrach Minkins: From Fugitive Slave to Citizen* (Cambridge: Harvard University Press, 1998).
15. On the Sims case, see Leonard W. Levy, "Sims' Case: The Fugitive Slave Law in Boston in 1851," *Journal of Negro History* 35:1 (January 1950), 39–74.

Chapter 9

1. Loguen, *The Rev. J. W. Loguen,* 409.
2. May, *Recollections,* 377.
3. *Syracuse Standard,* October 7, 17, and 20, and November 3, 1851.
4. William A. Graham, "Graham's Speech in Syracuse, May 20, 1851," in J. G. de Roulhac Hamilton, ed., *The Papers of William Alexander Graham,* vol. 4, 1851–1856 (Raleigh, NC: State Department of Archives and History, 1961), 98–102.
5. "Parish B. Johnson's Recollection," in Chase, *The Jerry Rescue,* 37–40.

6. *Syracuse Standard*, May 27, 1851; *Syracuse Star*, May 16, 1851. In his biography of Daniel Webster, Robert Remini discusses Webster's struggle with drinking during his last years. Robert Remini, *Daniel Webster: The Man and His Time* (New York: W. W. Norton & Co., 1997), 682.

7. *Syracuse Standard*, January 18, 1851.

8. See, for example, *Syracuse Star*, October 23, 1851.

9. "Tales of the Early Days," in *Syracuse Sunday Herald*, December 3, 1882.

10. Loguen, *The Rev. J. W. Loguen*, 397.

11. *Syracuse Standard*, November 6, 1850.

12. *Liberator*, January 3, 1851.

13. *New York Tribune*, January 11 and 14, 1851; *North Star*, January 16, 1851.

14. *Syracuse Standard*, March 6, 1851; *Liberator*, March 21, 1851.

15. *Liberator*, April 11, 1851.

16. *Syracuse Standard*, May 8, 1851.

17. May, *Recollections*, 134.

18. Webster, *Writings and Speeches*, 419–20.

Chapter 10

1. *Frederick Douglass' Paper*, October 9, 1851.

2. Diane Barnes, *Frederick Douglass: Reformer and Statesman* (New York: Routledge, 2013), 74.

3. Ibid.

4. Ibid.

5. *Syracuse Standard*, January 18, 1851.

6. See accounts of the hearing and subsequent events in U.S. Circuit Court, Special Term, Albany, January 26, 1853 in *Frederick Douglass' Paper*, February 4 and 11, 1853; Galpin, "The Jerry Rescue," 22–29; Sperry, "The Jerry Rescue," 25–27; Gurney S. Strong, *Early Landmarks of Syracuse* (Syracuse: The Times Publishing Company, 1894), 281–289.

7. *Frederick Douglass' Paper*, October 9, 1851.

8. *New York Tribune*, October 4, 1851.

9. *Frederick Douglass' Paper*, October 8, 1851.

10. "Mrs. Lucy Watson's Statement, 1894," in Chase, *The Jerry Rescue*, 43–44; *Syracuse Standard*, January 28, 1900.

11. Ella B. Moffet, "Jerry's Rescue—The Story," in *Syracuse Herald*, November 1, 1898; Loguen, *The Rev. J. W. Loguen*, 421–22.

12. Loguen, *The Rev. J. W. Loguen*, 423.
13. May, *Recollections*, 377–8.
14. *Liberator*, October 17, 1851.
15. *Frederick Douglass' Paper*, October 9, 1851.

Chapter 11
1. Ellen Douglas (Birdseye) Wheaton, *The Diary of Ellen Birdseye Wheaton* (Boston: Privately Published, 1923), 91.
2. Ibid.
3. Ibid., 42.
4. Connors, *Crossroads in Time*, 50.
5. *Voice of the Fugitive*, November 5, 1851.
6. Ward, *Autobiography*, 127.
7. Wheaton, *Diary*, November 2, 1851.
8. This letter was made public and reprinted in New York newspapers. *New York Tribune*, October 28, 1851; *Syracuse Star*, November 3, 1851; *Syracuse Standard*, October 7, 1851.
9. *New York Tribune*, October 3, 1851.
10. *National Antislavery Standard*, October 9, 1851.
11. *New York Tribune*, October 22, 1851.
12. Wheaton, *Diary*, 91.
13. *Syracuse Standard*, October 10, 1851.
14. Ibid., October 14, 1851.
15. Ibid; *Frederick Douglass' Paper*, October 30, 1851; Ward, *Autobiography*, 128.
16. *National Era*, October 9, 1851.
17. *Frederick Douglass' Paper*, October 16, 1851.
18. *Syracuse Standard*, October 10 and 11, 1851.
19. *Syracuse Journal*, October 9, 1851; *Syracuse Standard*, October 11 and 15, 1851; "Speech of Rev. Samuel J. May, to the Convention of Citizens of Onondaga County," in *Legal and Moral Aspects of Slavery, Selected Essays* (New York: Negro Universities Press, 1969), 3–20.
20. *Syracuse Standard*, October 16, 1851.
21. Ibid., October 24 and November 1 and 28, 1851; *Frederick Douglass' Paper*, November 27, 1851; *New York Tribune*, November 12, 1851.
22. *Liberator*, October 17, 1851.
23. Ibid., November 28, 1851.
24. Wheaton, *Diary*, 93.
25. *Frederick Douglass' Paper*, December 25, 1851.

26. Charles Wheaton to Gerrit Smith, October 20, 1851, Gerrit Smith Papers, Special Collections Research Center, Syracuse University Library, Syracuse, NY.
27. Gerrit Smith to Alfred Conkling, October 17, 1851, Gerrit Smith Papers.
28. Charles Wheaton to Gerrit Smith, October 20, 1851.
29. *Frederick Douglass' Paper*, October 30, 1851.
30. Charles Wheaton to Gerrit Smith, October 20, 1851.
31. Ibid.
32. *New York Tribune*, October 23, 1851.
33. *Liberator*, October 17, 1851; *New York Tribune*, November 3, 1851.
34. Quoted in Gurney S. Strong, *Early Landmarks of Syracuse* (New York: Times Publishing, 1894), 289–90.
35. *Hannibal Journal and Union*, October 16, 1851, quoted in Dempsey, *Searching for Jim*, 189.
36. *Savannah Daily Morning News*, October 8, 1851; *Raleigh Register*, October 11, 1851; *Fayetteville Observer*, October 7, 1851.
37. Wheaton, *Diary*, 91–2.
38. *Syracuse Star*, October 2 and 3, 1851.
39. Ibid., October 20, November 1, 4, and 20, and December 3, 8, and 19, 1851.
40. *OHA Bulletin* (Syracuse: OHA, 1961), 5.
41. *Syracuse Star*, October 25, 1851.
42. *New York Tribune*, October 28, 1851.
43. *Syracuse Standard*, October 28, 1851.
44. Ibid., November 25, 1851.
45. Wheaton, *Diary*, 92.

Chapter 12
1. Loguen, *The Rev. J. W. Loguen*, 427–8.
2. *Syracuse Standard*, October 6, 1851.
3. *Frederick Douglass' Paper*, November 27, 1851.
4. *Liberator*, May 14, 1852.
5. *Frederick Douglass' Paper*, February 5, 1852.
6. *New York Tribune*, October 1, 1853.
7. Fehrenbacher, *The Slaveholding Republic*, 244.
8. *Frederick Douglass' Paper*, December 25, 1851.
9. "The Trial of Henry W. Allen, U.S. Deputy Marshal, for Kidnapping," Gerrit Smith Broadside and Pamphlet Collection, Syracuse

University Library, Special Collections Research Center, digital
edition, 10, 38.
10. Ibid., 96.
11. *Frederick Douglass' Paper*, January 8 and February 5, 1852.
12. *Syracuse Standard*, October 6, 1852; *New York Tribune*, October 6,
1852; *Frederick Douglass' Paper*, October 15, 1852.
13. *Syracuse Standard*, October 11, 1851, January 25, June 22, November 19
and 25, 1854, and May 7 and June 15, 1857.
14. *Syracuse Standard*, September 28, 1857.
15. *Syracuse Journal*, September 7, 1867.
16. Ibid., August, 26, 1860.
17. Ibid., March 31, 1860; *Liberator*, April 27, 1860.

Chapter 13
1. *Syracuse Standard*, October 18, 1853.
2. R. E. Wheeler to President of the Onondaga Historical Association,
February 27, 1925, OHA.
3. *Syracuse Standard*, November 25, 1852.
4. Ibid., October 17, 1853.
5. Dick Case, *Good Guys, Bad Guys, Big Guys, Little Guys: Upstate
New York Stories from the Syracuse Herald-Journal, Herald American*
(Syracuse Newspapers, 1995), 184–187.
6. *Voice of the Fugitive*, February 26, 1852.
7. For examples see *Liberator*, November 19, 1852, April 29, 1853, and
October 23, 1857.
8. Ibid., November 19, 1852; *Frederick Douglass' Paper*, October 5, 1855.
9. *Liberator*, September 24, 1852.
10. *Frederick Douglass' Paper*, October 8, 1852.
11. Ibid., September 9, 1853.
12. *New York Tribune*, September 15, 1854.
13. *Frederick Douglass' Paper*, October 8 and 15, 1852; *Pennsylvania
Freeman*, October 16, 1852.
14. *Liberator*, October 15, 1852.
15. Ibid., October 21, 1853.
16. *Syracuse Standard*, October 2, 1854.
17. *Liberator*, March 30, 1855; *Frederick Douglass' Paper*, September 28,
1855.
18. *Liberator*, October 19, 1855.
19. *Carson League*, October 7, 1852; *Liberator*, November 19, 1852.

20. On the Anthony Burns case, see Earl M. Maltz, *Fugitive Slave on Trial: The Anthony Burns Case and Abolitionist Outrage* (Lawrence: University of Kansas Press, 2010); Albert von Frank, *The Trials of Anthony Burns: Freedom and Slavery in Emerson's Boston* (Cambridge: Harvard University Press, 1998).
21. *Syracuse Journal*, October 2, 1854.
22. Ibid., October 2, 1855; *Frederick Douglass' Paper*, October 5, 1855; *Liberator*, October 12, 1855.
23. *New York Tribune*, September 15, 1854.
24. *Syracuse Standard*, October 2, 1854.
25. *Frederick Douglass' Paper*, September, 28, 1855.
26. For more on "Bleeding Kansas" see Nicole Etcheson, *Bleeding Kansas: Contested Liberty in the Civil War Era* (Lawrence: University Press of Kansas, 2004); On the Brooks-Sumner incident see Williamjames Hull Hoffer, *The Caning of Charles Sumner: Honor, Idealism, and the Origins of the Civil War* (Baltimore: John Hopkins University Press, 2010).
27. *Syracuse Standard*, August 30, 1856.
28. Ibid., October 23, 1857.

Chapter 14

1. *Liberator*, October 23, 1857.
2. On the Republican Party, see Eric Foner, *Free Soil, Free Labor, Free Men: The Ideology of the Republican Party before the Civil War* (New York: Oxford University Press, 1971).
3. *Liberator*, October 23, 1857.
4. *New York Herald*, September 5, 1859.
5. Ibid., October 20, 1859; *The Charleston Mercury*, October 26, 1859.
6. For more on John Brown and his allies see Benjamin Quarles, *Allies for Freedom* and *Blacks on John Brown* (New York: Oxford University Press, 1974); Edward J. Renehan, Jr., *The Secret Six: The True Tale of the Men Who Conspired with John Brown* (Columbia: University of South Carolina Press, 1997).
7. *Liberator*, October 19, 1860.
8. Abraham Lincoln, "First Inaugural Address, March 4, 1861," in *The American Civil War: An Anthology of Essential Writings*, ed. Ian Frederick Finseth (New York: Taylor and Francis, 2006), 42; Harry V. Jaffa, *A New Birth of Freedom: Abraham Lincoln and the Coming of the Civil War* (Lanham, MD: Rowman & Littlefield Publishers,

2000), 264–67. For an excellent discussion of Abraham Lincoln's position on slavery, see also Eric Foner, *The Fiery Trial: Abraham Lincoln and American Slavery* (New York: W. W. Norton & Co., 2010).

9. *Liberator*, October 19, 1860.

10. *Fayetteville Observer*, December 13, 1859.

11. See "Declaration of the Immediate Causes which Induce and Justify the Secession of South Carolina from the Federal Union, December 24, 1860," in John Amasa May and John Reynolds Faunt, *South Carolina Secedes* (Columbia: University of South Carolina Press, 1960), 76–81; "Declaration of the Immediate Causes which Induce and Justify the Secession of the State of Mississippi from the Federal Union, 1861," in *Journal of the State Convention* (Jackson, MS: E. Barksdale, State Printer, 1861), 86–88; "Declaration of Causes for Secession for the State of Georgia, January 29, 1861," in *Official Records*, Series IV, Vol. 1, 81–88; "A Declaration of the Causes which Impel the State of Texas to Secede from the Federal Union, February 2, 1861," in E. W. Winkler, ed., *Journal of the Secession Convention of Texas*, 61–66.

12. Loguen, *The Rev. J. W. Loguen*, 444.

INDEX

....